A SIN BY
ANY OTHER
NAME

A SIN BY ANY OTHER NAME

RECKONING WITH RACISM AND THE HERITAGE OF THE SOUTH

Robert W. Lee IV

convergent
new york

Published in the United States by Convergent Books,
an imprint of the Crown Publishing Group,
a division of Penguin Random House LLC, New York.
convergentbooks.com

CONVERGENT BOOKS is a registered trademark and its
C colophon is a trademark of Penguin Random House LLC.

Library of Congress Cataloging-in-Publication Data
is available upon request.

ISBN 978-0-525-57638-9
Ebook ISBN 978-0-525-57639-6

PRINTED IN THE UNITED STATES OF AMERICA

Book design by Andrea Lau
Jacket design by Jessie Bright
Jacket photograph by

1 3 5 7 9 10 8 6 4 2

First Edition

To Mom and Dad: Thank you for your love.
You have shown me a sense of place, grace,
and hope while not conforming to our history,
and for that I remain forever grateful.

To Professor Jonathan L. Walton, Bertha, Gil,
Cody, and Josh Hamilton, and in faithful memory of
Gilbert Hamilton, who collectively changed how I view
race, the South, and everything we hold dear down here:
You are the reason I committed pen to paper;
you are all saints of a living God.

Sometimes it is necessary to reteach a thing its loveliness.

—GALWAY KINNELL

The Reverend Dr. Bernice A. King

I AM IN awe of God our Father and the truth of His Word. His ways are not our ways, and His thoughts are not our thoughts. For example, who could have imagined that a descendant of Confederate general Robert E. Lee, a man of war who owned slaves, and a descendant of Martin Luther King, Jr., a prophet who nonviolently fought for freedom and peace, would be connected for the cause of standing against systemic racism and working toward justice, equity, and peace? I don't think that any of us saw this coming but God.

I am honored to write the foreword for this book, because I believe that God is still at work for the cause of racial reconciliation. In April 1963, my father wrote to the clergy his "Letter from Birmingham Jail." Now, fifty-five years later, Robert W. Lee IV, a descendant of General

Robert E. Lee, has written the love letter to the church and to the South that you now hold in your hands. Both my father's letter and Robert's book deal with racism in America and point to our need for racial reconciliation.

Before Robert or I were born, my father prayed the following: "God grant that the people of good will would rise up with courage, take over the leadership, and open channels of communication between races, for I think that one of the tragedies of our whole struggle is that the South is still trying to live in monologue rather than dialogue." Perhaps for such a time as this, in answer to my father's prayer, God has raised up Robert W. Lee IV to join the cause of opening "the channels of communication between races." Sadly, but truthfully, the 2017 event in Charlottesville opened our eyes to see just how bad things still are in America with regard to race relations. For this cause, Robert W. Lee IV courageously spoke up on a global stage. This clearly wasn't easy, and it cost him dearly.

I know from experience that being courageous comes with a cost. On April 4, 2018, the world commemorated the fiftieth anniversary of the assassination of my father. My father had great love for God and humanity. His life was a living epistle that echoed Jesus's words from the Sermon on the Mount: "Love your enemies, bless those who curse you, do good to those who hate you, and pray for those who spitefully use you and persecute you." My father was chosen by God to live out this word in the twentieth century, and he obediently carried out his assignment.

Armed only with the love of God and the Holy Spirit, he fought courageously and nonviolently to help bring about change.

He was assassinated because of fear and indifference. Fear, because people were afraid that his challenge to racial and economic inequity would cost them their power. Indifference, because too many good people stayed silent in the face of hate, systemic racism, and unjust acts. But we thank God that the story does not end there. The assassin's bullet may have killed my father, but it did not stop or kill the good work that God started through him. The Bible tells us in Philippians 1:6, "He who has begun a good work in you will complete it until the day of Jesus Christ." When God begins a good work, He will raise up whomever He chooses to continue and complete it.

My mother once said, "Struggle is a never-ending process, and freedom is never really won; you earn it and win it in every generation." In the spirit of those words, I am so glad that God placed Robert W. Lee IV in this generation and moved him to join us in this struggle. As you read *A Sin by Any Other Name,* you will see that as a child, Robert did not see himself as being called to the cause of advancing freedom and racial reconciliation. Nevertheless, God chose him for the assignment.

The same has been true in my journey. Even though my parents were iconic nonviolent leaders, I did not see myself doing what I now know I have been called to do: serving as a bridge builder between the generations and continuing to advance the work that my parents began. I was only five years old when my father was assassinated, so I did not remember him as the leader of the civil rights movement. Most of what I learned about my father and his work came from my mother, who, in our home, consistently talked to my siblings and me about who he was. I also learned about my father through conversations with others who knew him well, and, ultimately, as I grew older, through his words, books, and speeches. God chose my mother to make sure that Daddy's words and speeches remained available, not just for me and my siblings, but for the world. I am forever grateful to God that she diligently and faithfully carried out her assignment.

The work of carrying on my parents' legacy of love and nonviolence didn't come easily for me. Because my father was killed by a white man, at one point in my life, I hated white men. But God had a different plan for me. He put several white men on my life's path to show me kindness. From those experiences and others, I came to see that what my father said is true: "Hate is too great a burden to bear" and "Men hate each other because they fear each other. They fear each other because they don't know each other, and they don't know each other because they don't communicate with each other, and they don't communicate with each other because they are separated from each other." In order to tear down the walls of hatred and fear, we must begin to communicate with one another and understand each other so that we can work together to eliminate systemic and institutional racism.

Like my father, some of us are called to communicate with the masses, but I believe that all of us are called to communicate with one another. At the King Center, we began a series called "The Beloved Community Talks," in which we bring together voices with different points of view to have courageous conversations about various issues impacting our communities, nation, and world, with the expressed purpose of bridging the divide. It was God's timing, and so appropriate, that Robert was able to join the Beloved Community Talks of 2018, where we focused on man's role and responsibility in bridging the racial divide.

Ultimately, though, transformational public dialogues must be accompanied by one-on-one talks around our dining room tables, in which parents communicate with their children and neighbors communicate with neighbors. An essential part of my father's development took place around his family's dining room table, where he and his siblings were able to talk with, learn from, and relate to others for growth and change; as you read this book, you will see through Robert's courageous stories that this is also what happened with him. His learning and development took place through transformational conversations in which he got to know and love African American women like Mrs. Janie, Mrs. Bertha, and others. Those seemingly little but significant one-on-one encounters with those ladies led to the larger conversations that Robert is now having as he speaks with leaders, influencers, and ordinary people all across America.

Despite the troubling persistence of racism in America today, I have hope, because God is still at work. Let's all join Him at the table of dialogue with one another, so that we can tear down the walls of racism, one person at a time, which can lead to bridging the racial divide and the realization of the Beloved Community.

THE REVEREND DR. BERNICE A. KING

CEO, THE KING CENTER

INTRODUCTION

W HEN I WAS YOUNG, I knew that my family had a famous relative, even if I didn't quite grasp what it meant. I remember being confused when my parents said we lived in the South even though our state, North Carolina, had "North" right in its name. But as I grew up in a culture steeped with Southern pride, eventually things fell into place. I am a nephew, generations removed, of Robert E. Lee, the general who led the armed forces of the Confederate States of America during the Civil War. Or the War of Northern Aggression. Or the Great Rebellion. As you'll see, it's complicated down here—especially when you're a Lee.

As a kid, I remember visiting Arlington House, Lee's homestead just across the river from the White House, and feeling starstruck knowing I was related to the man who'd lived on that sprawling estate. I even bought a photo of the general—Uncle Bob, as we called him—and a replica of the flag for which he fought, and hung them on the wall of my bedroom. Once I entered high school, the relationship became more fraught. By then, I had realized that my name carried more weight than most. People would sometimes project on to me their own problematic views. Even now, when I hand my credit card to a cashier, it's not unusual for them to ask in awed tones if I'm related to "him." Sometimes they'll even say, "The South will rise again," assuming they've found a fellow patriot. They haven't.

After college, I responded to a call to ministry and found myself working at a small church in North Carolina. Then Charlottesville happened. As hundreds of angry young white men—people who looked just like me—marched through the otherwise bucolic college town, wielding tiki torches that lit up the hate on their faces, I realized I needed to do my part in confronting our country's stain of race-based violence with a strong and certain voice. I owed it to the women of color who had taken time from their lives to help me learn the faith. That the controversy at the heart of the Charlottesville rally was a statue honoring General Robert E. Lee only added to my sense of urgency. So I choked down my fear and used my voice, arguing that the statue of my ancestor must come down in order for our society to move forward on the issue of race.

That's when the headlines appeared. Interview requests poured in, and I ended up appearing on the MTV Video Music Awards, of all places. The glitz of A-list musicians isn't really my scene, but meeting Susan Bro sticks with me to this day. Susan's daughter, Heather Heyer, was the young social justice activist killed during the violence in Charlottesville. Onstage at the VMAs, Susan stood tall and pleaded with viewers to carry on Heather's quest for justice—just fifteen days after her daughter's death. In the year since that moment, I've been able to travel the country, meeting other inspiring leaders who are calling for justice in a time when such work, for various reasons, has become increasingly risky.

My own entry into this world of public theology is something of an accident, owing to a distant relative with whom I share a first and last name. But it hasn't been without challenges. Life in a small Southern town will do that, especially when you challenge the status quo.

My hometown of Statesville, North Carolina, is a lot like the fictional town of Pawnee, Indiana, the setting of NBC's hit show *Parks and Recreation*. Like Pawnee, we have resilient citizens who are convinced that their little, unremarkable plot of land—in this case, twenty-four square miles at the intersection of Interstate 77 and Interstate 40—is the best part of the Southern part of God's country. Take, for instance, a column by Joe Hudson published in our hometown newspaper, the *Statesville Record and Landmark*:

We're a modest little city of 25,000 friends and neighbors located north of the quasi-nation city of Charlotte, which as you may have heard, is a cultural mecca and one of the greatest banking centers in the free world.

Statesville is not. . . .

Charlotte consumes gallons of vinaigrette dressings and tons of smoked salmon. Statesville is a city where fish is fried (as our Lord intended they be) and a bottle of Kraft French Dressing is good enough for anybody—so get over yourself. Oh sure, we have restaurants that can compete on a global scale with any plate of pâté or crème de menthe cake you would want, but to go into detail would be bragging and unfair to others, especially to New York. We're too modest for that.

I, too, love Statesville, but I don't look at the town in the same way I once did. It's not the happy-go-lucky Pawnee portrayed on television. There are deep chasms of race and class and income that divide our community—and sometimes, most visibly, our churches. At the same time, it was people in Statesville who encouraged me to look beyond these challenges and see that there is something in the South worth fighting for. Our churches and neighborhoods may be unofficially segregated, but if you venture beyond these systemic boundaries, Statesville is filled with deeply faithful women and men living out the Gospel message of love.

They are the people who spend their weekends sharpening their disaster relief skills at a local church, so they will be prepared to help out in the aftermath of a bad summer storm. Or the real-life Good Samaritan who, when she found a gentleman who had fallen into a ditch while riding a lawnmower, helped out herself instead of waiting for someone else to jump in. And the couple who won $250,000 on a scratch-off lottery ticket, and instead of buying new cars or taking vacations, are planning to open a center to help people struggling from addiction. These are all things that happened in my hometown in the past few months, reminders that despite the bad news we read about in the paper, there are still many points of light here. That's why I'm proud to call Statesville home.

Likewise, I love the fact that I have been part of a family that has helped shape this nation. But it hasn't been without challenges. Too often, I've been asked why I just don't change my name if I'm so hell-bent on changing how we view things. First of all, it's part of who I am. Secondly, the Lee family legacy runs deeper than the actions of my distant uncle. Two Lees signed the Declaration of Independence and fought in our nation's Revolution. That being said, I recognize the fact that the most famous Lee, a man by the name of Robert, used his power, reputation, and prestige to betray his nation in a way that few ever could.

What you hold in your hands is a memoir with a mission. I'm twenty-six years old, and if I play my cards right, I have time left to tell more stories and make more memories. But that doesn't change the fact that in August 2017, our collective world changed because my distant ancestor had been made into an idol of white supremacy. As a member of the Lee family, I share my story in hopes that it will help others see that the dismantling of this idolatry will leave the South stronger in its loveliness, not weaker.

There's only one way out of this mess, one way to bend toward justice, and that is together. Time and time again, women and men have intervened in my life and shown me a different way of living together in a community like Statesville. My family background is unique, but my journey isn't. Stories like mine can be found throughout the South, and I have no doubt that countless other young white Southerners will be able to relate to the complexities of growing up in this beautiful if flawed region. Yet I truly believe that part of the beauty of this place exists in its resilience and its ability to change. Even if it hasn't reached its full potential yet.

The stories in this book are presented as I remember them. If I have omitted anyone or anything, or misremembered a detail here and there, I apologize. I share them not to wag a finger at the South, but to reckon with the double-edged sword of the South's sense of place, and with God's abiding presence in it all. There is no excuse for some of the behavior in this book, some of which I committed. But I hope that by being honest about my own experiences, I can prompt some moments of reflection that lead to a precious, deep, and abiding hope for the atonement for our past.

Our beauty here in the South is found in so many things: culture, song, food—especially biscuits—religion, the strong branches of the magnolia tree I climbed as a child, the red clay of the Piedmont, and so much more. There is much to celebrate, and I hope some of my fondness for my home is evident. But undergirding our culture is the sin of white privilege and racism—especially in the white church. As a pastor, it's my job to notice these things and call them what they are. For a sin by any other name is still a sin.

1

He's an on-time God, yes he is.

—DOTTIE PEOPLES

I WAS ABOUT TO take the stage at the annual Martin Luther King, Jr., breakfast in Statesville when Mother Aleen Alexander caught my eye and motioned for me to join her at her table. When I made my way over, she took my clammy hands—nerves from anticipating the speech I was about to deliver—and looked into my eyes.

"Darkness is after you," she said.

I come from a mainline Protestant tradition that puts little stock in warnings of spirits and evil. Talk of darkness as a supernatural force isn't something I'm accustomed to, but in the years that I have known Mother Aleen, I've recognized that there is something of the prophetic within her, a rare connection to God. When she speaks in this way, I know in my gut she's probably right.

"Today is the start of something you've never expected,"

she continued, unfazed by my fidgeting. "You don't know what the future holds, but God does, and God has plans for you to bridge a gap."

The "today" she referenced was my speech at that morning's breakfast. I was nervous, unsure why a twenty-four-year-old white minister with limited life experience had been invited to keynote an event that saw the town's political and civic leaders—black and white—come together for at least one morning of peaceful bread breaking each year. The column I regularly wrote in the *Statesville Record and Landmark* was sometimes devoted to issues of justice, not always the easiest topic to cover down here. That column had caught the eyes of some local African American activists in town, who invited me to attend an interfaith prayer service at the First Baptist Church, Incorporated, one of two First Baptist Churches in town. It's nonsensical to have two First Baptists in a single community, until you realize they are divided between white and black Christians. That we continue to accept this as normal shows how much more work we have to do as white Southern Christians to heal the wounds of our racist past. In my column and sermons, I had been advocating for greater relationships between our white and black churches. Deacon William Jones, an activist involved with the local chapter of the NAACP, reached out through a close friend and asked if I might be interested in joining the MLK breakfast.

This was the first time I would speak, rather than

write, about race publicly in my hometown. I planned to highlight some of the heroes whose words and actions had prompted me to reflect deeply about the culture of the South, and how that culture had formed my views on race. Statesville is a place I love deeply; it is where the seeds of my faith were planted, where my vocation as a minister was fostered. But it's also a place that I realize has failed to live up to its own ideals.

Mother Aleen's words that morning threw me for a loop, but I tried not to spend too much time thinking of them. I had a speech to give. As I walked up the stairs to the platform, I paused and surveyed the crowd of about six hundred people from the community. When I glanced down at the table where Mother Aleen sat, I saw that her head was down and her lips were moving. She was praying for me.

I inhaled deeply and began my talk.

"If black lives don't matter now, when will they matter at all?" I preached. "I've been frustrated with the lack of trust and civility between those in public trust and persons of color, between Muslims and Christians, between Republicans and Democrats. We have forsaken our most sacred values as a nation for the sake of separation and for assimilation."

A few "amens" went up from the crowd. I relaxed. This was as friendly and supportive an audience I'd find. The encouragement was coming more from the black people in the audience than the white people, which is rather typical of Statesville even now. "We want to talk about race. We want to confront this. Now is the time to confront racism for what it is," I continued. A few more "amens," some applause. I glanced at Mother Aleen. She was still praying.

"If not now, when will we have sensible and attainable education goals within our community, our nation, and our world? If not now, when will we call to task our elected leaders for their racist policies that systematically oppress persons of color? If not now, when will we engage in the hard work of truth telling that seeks to put an end to systematic forms of racism in our city square? In moments like these, we need twenty-first-century courage. We need to be people who stare racism in the face and say, 'You may be great, but I know a God who is greater.'"

When I finished, I headed back to that table to hug my then-fiancée, Stephanie, and ask Mother Aleen what she thought of the speech.

"This is the start of something big," she said.

IT WAS NEVER a blinding light nor a single moment that changed my views of the South. Our region's attitude toward race can be obscured, hidden behind our polite veneer. But the reality is, our schools and churches remain largely segregated, and it isn't uncommon to hear the N-word coming from the lips of white Christians. Often there's a sad acceptance of the status quo, a resignation that things just won't get better. But for me, ordinary moments like the one with Mother Aleen hold the power of conversion. Only in hindsight do those grace-filled encounters add up to reveal God's work in our lives.

In the Bible, there's a story where Jesus comes alongside two of his disciples as they walk the road to Emmaus. At first, the disciples don't recognize the risen Lord, but he opens the scriptures to his friends, unconcerned that they were initially blind to who he really was. Similarly, Mother Aleen is one of many people who have helped me see the challenges that remain in terms of racial justice, the school-to-prison pipeline, the segregation of our town, and the Confederate monument that sits near our city square. These people have encouraged me to use my voice to do my part. They have shown me the heart of God and the heart of what it means to be a white person in the South.

Our experiences in the South must be told anew. On the good days, these stories intertwine and work together to weave a tapestry as beautiful as the stars and lightning bugs on a summer evening in North Carolina. But they also tell the story of hatred, white supremacy, and fear. We balance these two realities here in the South, and it is my hope that the stories of grace will ultimately come out triumphant. In my own journey, the moments of transformation have come because people of color had the patience to translate to me the song in the heart of God. But recently I've come to believe that it is incumbent upon white people like me to "get our own folk" to confront our own power and privilege. There is truth in the statement that once you have seen something, you can't unsee it.

The speech I gave at the Statesville Civic Center took place months before Mother Aleen's words would begin to make sense to me. She said them to me, her hands holding mine, long before the hideous marches in Charlottesville that saw white-hot hatred spill into the streets and kill a peaceful counterprotester, and well before I realized that my family's connection to General Robert E. Lee gave me a platform and credibility to speak out and be listened to by white people—to confront the racist structures my fore-bears fought to prop up.

Shortly after those events, when the hate mail started to pour in and I left the North Carolina church where I'd held my first job as a solo pastor, the darkness Mother Aleen predicted felt more real than I ever imagined. So I focused on the second part of her message: God has a plan for me. I'm starting to believe that despite the darkness, moments of grace extended to me, like the one on that day in the Statesville Civic Center, are what defines us. But in order to recognize and appreciate these moments of grace, we must listen with the ear of our heart, as Saint Benedict put it.

I am a Lee who feels my family has done our fair share of talking. Even this book may come off as more commentary from my family. Now, it's time to listen, so that the many moments of grace don't elude us, but serve to inspire us to usher in God's reign.

2

O, God of dust
And rainbows,
Help us see
That without the dust
The rainbow
Would not be.

—LANGSTON HUGHES

HANGING ON A wall in my grandmother's den
is a painting of General Robert E. Lee. It's been
there as long as I can remember, as familiar to me as her
1970s-era shag carpet and the metallic-green artificial
Christmas tree that appears in her home each December.
The painting depicts Lee surrounded by a dozen or so ad-
miring officers. His expression is deep and somber, all his
men turned to him as if to ask, "What's next?"

Even as a young child, there was something about this
painting that attracted me. Whereas other depictions of
Lee turned me off with their over-the-top militarism, this

particular portrait stirred within me a sense of duty, patriotism, and adventure. Next to the painting is a couch where as children we would cozy up to my nana, Barbara Lee. If we were lucky, she would tell us stories about her life, and, on rare occasions, stories about our ancestors.

Nana has a story for everything. With stately red hair and a seemingly endless supply of energy, she was always a fascinating figure to us kids. She founded and has belonged to the same bridge club for more than five decades. She was president of the Garden Club of North Carolina and CFO of the manufacturing company our family owned. One time, she hosted Princess Anne at a luncheon. Even at home, Nana has always been the quintessential Southern lady, always put together in a skirt and matching top. As children, our time with her gave us insight into the Southern heritage that shaped generations of our family—and I was always eager to learn more.

One afternoon a couple of decades ago, Nana called me into the den and asked me to sit down on the couch. Her request wasn't unusual—we had spent countless hours together in this room—but even as a young boy of about five I could sense that something important was about to take place. I climbed up on the couch and watched Nana walk over to a rolltop desk that contained the family marriages, lineage, and history; it's contained in a thick, leather-bound book that holds the records for the generations of our family. The adults usually took it out when they needed to look something up, a question about an ancestor, social security number, or some uncertainty about the date of a wedding or a death. But for us kids, that book was something mysterious, belonging to the realm of adults. And now it was my turn with this impressive book.

Nana sat down on the couch, placed the records on her lap, and thumbed through pages that were transcribed in careful penmanship. She carefully pulled out a white envelope that contained many sheets of papers and, one by one, began showing them to me and reading off the names of people from a distant past.

"You come from a long line of people who have been in this country for a very long time," she explained. "These names might not mean much to you now, but someday they will."

I looked up at her quizzically. "Like Uncle John?" I said, recognizing one of the Lee names she read aloud.

"No, much older," she said. "These were people who lived a long time ago."

"When?" I asked.

"Well, you are Robert W. Lee IV, which means there were many other Robert Lees before you," she explained patiently. "The original Lees came to Virginia and then made their way down to Alabama. Some of those Lees came back here to North Carolina."

I looked confused, like I still didn't get it. So she pointed across the room.

"See that painting over there, the one of General Lee on the horse?"

I nodded.

"You are related to him, a nephew separated by many generations," she explained.

That did it. I may not have understood what "ancestry" meant, how I was an indirect or collateral descendant, as some call it, or why the Lee clan made their way from Virginia down to Alabama and back to North Carolina in the first place. But I understood I was related to someone important.

"So we're famous?" I asked excitedly.

"Not quite," she replied. "It's complicated."

As a child, the weight of those words was lost on me. All I remember was feeling so happy to be snuggled next to Nana, learning about our family and finding out that some of its members had done things that were worth putting down in a book.

Over the next several years, as I came of age in a culture soaked with reverence for our Confederate past, I would begin to idolize Lee. This is pretty much a given for a white child of the South. Our streets are named for him, and our parks contain statues depicting him. Plus, I was one of the lucky ones related to him. How could I not be proud?

Ultimately, though, the presence of this man in Southern life goes beyond family ties. It's hard to overstate what a hero this controversial ancestor of mine continues to be for many people in the South today. More than a handful of counties, stretching from Florida to Texas, are named for Lee, as are a couple dozen public schools. There are even more parkways named for him, along with a seemingly countless number of monuments, markers, and statues. To outsiders, those who didn't breathe in the Lee lore from childhood, it might seem mystifying.

Take the story of one elementary school in a black neighborhood of Amarillo, Texas, which for six decades has been called Robert E. Lee Elementary School. (Texas is its own thing, and this boy from the Old North State won't pretend to be able to explain life in the Lone Star State. But affinity for Lee is everywhere in the South, Texas included.) In 2017, a group of parents and community activists asked the school board to change the name of the school, pointing out that young black children might be uncomfortable learning in a building named for a Confederate general. Other schools in the district had been named for the neighborhood where they were located, so the parents of Lee Elementary asked that the school follow the same protocol.

But it wasn't that easy. Some in the community said that changing the name would be a concession to creeping political correctness, which is usually what people say when they don't want to admit that part of their culture is actually problematic to others. They pointed to Lee's history, which included playing a major role in securing Texas for the United States from Mexico, and said that Lee must be seen for more than his connection to the Confederacy. Emotions ran wild, and the school board meetings were heated. In the end, the board handed down a split decision that offered something of a bizarre compromise. The name would be changed to Lee Elementary School, with the "Robert E." chopped off.

To outsiders like my wife and her family, who hail from Massachusetts, fights like these can seem bizarre. How could anyone think it's a good idea to educate young black children in a school named for a man who led the charge to preserve slavery? Well, half of Amarillo did, according to a poll published by a local paper. The Lee legend continues to pervade the South.

Even Lee's detractors must admit that he led a thoroughly remarkable life. The Lee family traces our roots back to the American Revolution, and Lees held many important posts in our nation's history. Robert E. Lee's father, for example, was a trusted aide to President George Washington, who paid personal visits to the Lee home.

While the younger Lee's early career in the U.S. Army wasn't particularly notable, at least combat-wise, he became a master of what we now call civil engineering and strategy. His most significant engineering achievement opened up the mighty Mississippi to increased shipping from large boats. Later, he helped defend the United States from attacks by Native Americans, a feat widely praised at the time (though really it was an invasion of Native Americans' sacred homeland). He took part in the Mexican-American War, a campaign he later said he regretted, given the imbalance of power between the two nations. Still, "manifest destiny" was the U.S. mantra in those years, and Lee was a man of his time.

Southern children learn from a young age that Lee was a class act, a Southern gentleman and master tactician, that both President Lincoln and President Davis asked him to lead their military forces at the start of the Civil War. Children learn that Lee, a religious man, spent much time in prayer agonizing over his decision. The legend goes that Mary Lee heard her husband pacing upstairs, ruminating over what to do, before dropping to his knees in prayer, unable to decide whether he should stick with the nation he had served for decades or walk away to defend his beloved home state. Finally, General Lee walked downstairs and informed his wife that he was a Virginian first, and he had a duty to protect the commonwealth from federal interference. In other words, General Lee took the view that his identity as a son of Virginia was more important to him than his citizenship of the United States. That view was ubiquitous back then in the South, and it maintains some popularity even today, even among those who find Lee's actions reprehensible.

Southerners are always reframing our history, responding to challenges from those who seek to show how brutality shaped life in the antebellum South. This willful ignorance is played out every day, from school classrooms to office watercoolers, producing an interpretation of history that ignores the sin and damage of chattel slavery.

Even how we name the war that split the South from

the North shows how complicated this history is. In the decades following the Civil War, the U.S. government referred to the conflict as "the War of Rebellion," as Chandra Manning and Adam Rothman reported in the *New York Times*. The U.S. government had reason to frame the conflict in this way, which suggested that the South had been co-opted by a group of rebels who had to be put down. But as time went on, the South sought to reframe what happened. Jefferson Davis, the onetime president of the Confederate States of America, began using the term "Civil War," which laid blame on both sides. By the late 1880s, Davis's term had taken over, only to be supplanted in the early 1900s by the even more neutral, "War Between the States." This phrase, and the more belligerent "War of Northern Aggression," are still common in the South today.

Even though Lee's legacy is sometimes debated here in the South, he does exemplify the attributes of a certain kind of antebellum Southern gentleman. Lee's admirers see a man of humility, elegance, and commitment to faith—a man who lived out the region's highest ideals. They note how when Lee took control of Virginia's army on April 23, 1861, less than two weeks after the Battle of Fort Sumter, he decided to forgo the fancy dress that someone of his rank could demand, instead donning a gray coat with leather riding pants and cowboy boots. No golden braids, medals, or ribbons to signify his status as the army's highest commander.

Even in defeat, some Southerners see in Lee a noble humility. At Appomattox, General Grant initially arranged a surrender that would allow Lee to avoid embarrassment by sending a subordinate to meet with Grant in his stead. But Lee, whose father had witnessed a similar arrangement play out in front of General Washington during the Revolution, rejected the plan. A true gentleman, Lee took responsibility for the military defeat by surrendering in person. A quiet power, a man often depicted deep in prayer—this is the Lee we Southern youth come to admire.

Notice that I didn't mention slavery in this depiction of Lee's life. That's because for Southerners, slavery is a secondary issue in the life of our greatest hero. Nearly everyone agrees that slavery was a horrific part of our past, but when it comes to Lee, we massage it away, telling ourselves that Lee himself abhorred slavery. We read and are taught that Lee wanted to free his slaves, including the two hundred that his wife inherited. We learn that Lee's son wrote fondly of a house slave who played a pivotal role in his life. We're taught that Lee and his wife set up a school on their estate, in violation of the law at the time, so that the slaves could receive some education before they were released.

But the facts speak for themselves. Lee profited enormously from slave labor and the abuse of enslaved persons. He oppressed and "owned" human beings—and though he did eventually release them, their freedom came just weeks before the Emancipation Proclamation was handed down, after Lee had subjected them to years of grueling work.

Here's another thing we don't learn—at least not if we want to feel comfortable accepting the benevolent picture of Lee I sketched above: Robert E. Lee held very racist views. In *Clouds of Glory,* a thorough, if somewhat sympathetic, biography, the historian Michael Korda highlights a letter in which Lee suggests to his wife that slaves are "better off" in the United States than they would've been in Africa, a common view at the time. Of their suffering, Lee writes that the "painful discipline they are undergoing, is necessary for their instruction as a race, & I hope will prepare & lead them to better things." To Lee, slavery may have been evil, but it was a necessary evil. Slavery, he believed, would end when God was ready for human beings to stop owning one another. Until then, it was fair game.

Lee maintained his belief in white supremacy long after the Confederacy fell. He didn't think black people should vote. He thought the freed slaves should be returned to Africa, an arrangement he believed would be better for them and for the white people staying behind in the United States.

It is true that Lee was more complicated than the pictures both his fans and foes have painted. But the abhorrent facts of my ancestor's life are too often ignored by those with fondness for the South. It's time we look deeper into what we're honoring when we honor this man.

3

The ache for home lives in all of us. The safe place
where we can go as we are and not be questioned.

——MAYA ANGELOU

WHEN I WAS growing up, Statesville felt like
the ideal Southern town. Situated at the intersection of Interstates 77 and 40 in western North Carolina,
it bills itself as an All-American City and a city of progress. The town's origins go back to the eighteenth century, when Scots-Irish Protestants settled the area and
began cultivating the land for farming. Their hard work
paid off. A century later, the community became one of
North Carolina's biggest growers of tobacco, and home to
a healthy whiskey business. Generations later, when my
family arrived, the industries changed and plants started
to move overseas—Statesville adapted with the times, or
at least we tried.

When I was a child in the 1990s, Statesville was in the
midst of a boom, with the population surging more than

30 percent between 1990 and 2000, topping out at about twenty-four thousand people. About 60 percent of those residents were white, residing mainly on the north side of town, where my family lived. Nana and my dad owned a plant that made battery components, over on the south side. My brother, Scott, and I spent countless hours roaming the factory floor, blissfully unaware that it might not be the best playground for children.

During hot Southern summers, Scott and I rode our bikes through the predominantly black neighborhoods that surrounded the redbrick plant. When it got too cold to stay outside for long stretches, we'd play inside, running through what felt like a life-size maze created by the tall stacks of cardboard boxes, or watching TV in the office, plopped down in mini La-Z-Boy recliners that had been purchased specially for us. We would overhear Nana and my dad talking about business, which was still doing well in those days. Sometimes, when we were lucky, we would watch PBS documentaries about the history of the South, and especially the Civil War, on the office's box television. There was plenty of Thomas the Tank Engine, Mister Rogers, the Muppets, and of course *Star Trek*, too.

These lessons, whether from war documentaries or the wisdom of Fred Rogers, caused Scott and me to think deeply about where we came from. We had heard about the War of Northern Aggression, the Great Rebellion, and the Civil War, but it never occurred to us that all of these names referred to the same thing. We knew the importance of neighborly love, but we had no idea that our family had committed atrocious acts against the nation. We knew the Civil War was bloody and bad, but we were kids, too, full of hope and expectancy for what might be next on television after the Civil War documentary was over. The deeper reckoning with our sense of place and our family's role in our country's painful past would happen over the course of a lifetime.

At the end of the workday, Dad would drive us home to a neighborhood that could have come straight out of a 1950s-era television sitcom. Our home was a well-kept split-level situated within the Statesville Country Club, in a nice part of town with lush lawns and flowering trees. My parents, knowing how much it would mean to their children, had also purchased the empty lot next door, providing my brother and I plenty of room to spend hours outside playing. In the warm months, we'd run around outside until Mom called us in for dinner—literally ringing a bell to summon us inside. When we got a little older, we convinced our dad to buy us dirt bikes. Making figure eights, we raced each other around the lot until the turf was torn to shreds and we ran out of gas. Other times, Scott and I would take the BB guns we'd been given for Christmas and shoot at various homemade targets. Our childhood was undeniably Southern, resembling a picturesque movie about small-town white folk. And I loved it.

ON SUNDAYS, our family worshipped at Broad Street United Methodist Church right in the center of town. I was baptized there on All Saints' Day, a liturgical holy day that still holds a special place in my heart. It was at Broad Street that I began to understand the value of Christian community and, later, where I began to see the challenges facing my hometown and my church. But as a child, what I remember most was feeling inspired by the beauty of the worship services and the majesty of the church building itself.

As you enter the sanctuary, your eyes are drawn up to a stunning Tiffany window that depicts an angel and the heavens. The window was saved from a fire that destroyed the original building at the turn of the twentieth century. Other magnificent stained-glass windows are situated throughout the church; when the sunlight is just right, streams of color flood the worship space, the brilliant white walls suddenly ablaze with reminders of God's knack for beauty.

The sanctuary where the congregation now gathers was built in 1909. Lees have worshipped there since the new building was erected, and my granddaddy has rung the bell in the church's magnificent tower since as far back as I can remember, calling people to prayer in a rich, deep B-flat.

My earliest memories of church come from the radio.

Early on, I never went to the main worship service—"big church," as we call it—because I was easily distracted during the sermon. Instead, Nana would take me home after Sunday school, and we'd listen on the radio. Whenever the congregation sang, I would try to pick out my parents' voices amid the sea of worshippers belting out the great hymns of the faith.

Around the age of ten, I remember skipping service altogether to run up and down the wheelchair ramp with my friends. It was an un-pious start for someone who would become an ordained minister, but it turns out it was actually the quintessential Lee way. When my dad was growing up, he skipped most services to play pool in the church basement with Linwood, the black sexton who cared for our facilities.

When I started attending worship regularly, I couldn't have been more than about eleven years old. But even then, I sensed that something was off. During our bike rides around Dad's plant, my brother and I frequently saw black kids outside playing or walking with their families. But at our Sunday services, everyone was white. I couldn't understand why our worship didn't reflect the world outside the walls of our magnificent Gothic church. It wasn't something I remember my family addressing, nor the pastors who preached from the pulpit. I'm not sure I even asked about it as a kid. We all just seemed to see it as just the way it was.

My first memory of this divide being addressed happened not at church, but around the family TV. One hot evening, late in the summer right before school was about to start, my dad and I walked downstairs to the den and sat down in the deep-brown leather recliners. He handed me an ice-cold glass bottle of Coca-Cola and flipped on the television. He had grown up watching the original *Star Trek* in the 1960s and he wanted to share that special part of his childhood with me. *Star Trek: The Next Generation* was playing in reruns, so he made sure that we caught as many episodes together as possible.

On this particular night, with my Coke in hand, the ice crystals stuck stubbornly to the bottle, the episode seemed heavier than the others. Called "The Measure of a Man," the plot finds Jean-Luc Picard, the captain of the USS *Enterprise*, engaged in a tense debate about the future of one of his officers, an android named Data. A Starfleet scientist wants to subject the robot to a series of experiments to understand how he was created, but there is a risk that these experiments could end up destroying Data. The officers on the *Enterprise* must decide: Should the experiments be allowed to proceed?

Midway through the episode, Captain Picard vents his frustration to Guinan, the bartender aboard the *Enterprise*, played by Whoopi Goldberg. Guinan is a mysterious character; little is known about her personal history, other than the fact that she is hundreds of years old and very close to Captain Picard. As the two talk about the dilemma,

Guinan makes the captain understand the serious moral questions about Data's case.

"Consider that in the history of many worlds, there have always been disposable creatures," she says matter-of-factly. "They do the dirty work. They do the work no one else wants to do because it's too difficult or it's too hazardous.

"And an army of Datas is all disposable," Guinan continues. "You don't have to think about their welfare. You don't think about how they feel. Whole generations of disposable people."

Picard, looking on uneasily as Guinan takes a sip of her drink, replies, "You're talking about slavery."

"Oh, I think that's a little harsh," she replies.

"I don't think that's a little harsh. I think that's the truth," Picard says. "But that's a truth we have obscured behind a comfortable, easy euphemism: 'property.' And that's not the issue at all, is it?"

I remember being confused by the exchange. People could use and throw away other people? It didn't make sense to me. With wide eyes, I looked over to dad.

"Could this really happen?" I asked him.

"It *has* happened," he told me.

Sensing that I wanted to know more, Dad turned down the television so we could talk.

"At one point in history, people treated other human beings as property," he said, slowly, considering his words. Slavery, I now realize, isn't the easiest topic to broach with a young kid. I stared in amazement: The concept of people thinking they owned other people was so foreign to me at the time that I didn't really believe him.

It would be years before I had to reckon with the fact that slave owners weren't just theoretical, confined to history or to television. Rather, my own family members had been among them, even the man whose portrait hung in Nana's den across town. But none of that came up as we sat in our own den that night.

I remember feeling scared, unable to understand how human beings could own and mistreat other people. It was that conversation, the first I ever had with a family member about slavery, that began to pit my childhood sense of justice against my family's Southern heritage.

4

"All I'm saying is, kindness don't have no boundaries."

—KATHRYN STOCKETT, *THE HELP*

FOR THE FIRST four years of my life, I was cared for by a woman named Janie Bowman while my parents were at work. My father was busy running the plant, and my mom was climbing the management ladder at Iredell Memorial Hospital. Seeking help, they reached out to Janie, a retired nurse my mother knew from work, and asked if she would be interested in watching me during the week. She was.

For several years, Janie had worked as a floor nurse at the hospital. Like nearly everything else in the South, medical care had once been officially segregated, with white and black residents of Iredell County using separate facilities to see their doctors. Iredell Memorial Hospital, as far as I can remember, had always been a place of great progress in the medical field, but I remember hearing stories that signs marking the separate entrances for white and "colored" people remained in place long after the laws were changed.

By the time I was born, legal segregation in Statesville was long a thing of the past, and so were many of the social structures that went along with it, including "hired help." And yet, there was Janie Bowman and a younger version of me, together in our little galley kitchen—a black nanny and a white toddler, in a scene that is still quite common in many Southern homes.

My earliest memories of Janie involved her cooking, singing, and praying. She would place me at the kitchen table and make her way over to the stove to prepare lunch. She limped visibly when she walked, each step evidence that her life hadn't always been easy. That limp would create a moment between us that planted seeds in my mind that something about life in the South was not as it should be. Or, as I believe still, as it could be.

Sometimes I'll see a visible marker of the South's overtly racist past, or read a news story about white supremacy going public yet again, and my thoughts go back to Janie. My memories of her are seared in my mind, as fresh today as if she were still with me in our den. She was always sporting a pair of those big, aviator-style glasses that were so popular in the nineties. She dressed impeccably, done up in the most professional of clothes even though she knew her day would be spent caring for a messy toddler, cooking meals, changing diapers, and even playing on the floor of our den. She slouched in her stance, not because of bad posture but because time had not been kind to her.

Janie Bowman was instrumental in forming my young Christian faith—and, ultimately, in my seeking ordination many years later. Whenever I was acting fussy or she thought I needed a break from the TV, she would turn off *Mister Rogers' Neighborhood* or the Muppets or *Thomas and Friends,* pull me up on her lap, and read to me from a well-worn leather-bound Bible. The Psalms were her favorite. She read the verses slowly, her voice rich and deep and filled with love. Other times, she would hold me close and sing softly, the music a clear expression of her quietly powerful faith. She had many favorite hymns, and I remember vividly Janie rocking me and gently singing "Sweet Hour of Prayer," the nineteenth-century hymn that remains popular among many Gospel choirs.

> *Sweet hour of prayer! Sweet hour of prayer!*
> *That calls me from a world of care,*
> *And bids me at my Father's throne*
> *Make all my wants and wishes known.*
> *In seasons of distress and grief,*
> *My soul has often found relief,*
> *And oft escaped the tempter's snare,*
> *By thy return, sweet hour of prayer!*

For Janie, the sweet hour of prayer animated her entire day. As a young kid, I looked up to her and wanted to be just like her. So much so, that it affected my stride as a toddler.

A little while after I started walking, my parents noticed that I, too, had started to limp. They couldn't figure out why. I had never broken a bone, and I had walked just fine a few days earlier. So they took me to a specialty shoe store to find out if I needed some kind of corrective footwear. No dice. Next they tried a podiatrist, who after a thorough examination assured my parents that nothing was wrong with me. "Your son should be able to walk fine," he told them. My mom and dad were puzzled. They hoped I'd grow out of it, but for now, there appeared to be nothing they could do.

One morning, while chatting with Janie, my mom and dad filled her in on the limp and asked if she had any idea what might be causing my condition.

"Ahhh," she said with a smile. "Give me a day and it'll be fixed."

My parents, exasperated by the situation, smiled and hoped that somehow, someway, Janie could fix the issue plaguing their young child.

Later that day, Janie noticed that my limp was on the same side as hers, and her suspicions were confirmed. I was mimicking the way she walked, part of my quest to be a mini Janie Bowman. I don't remember the specifics of what came next, but based on what my family has told me over the years, Janie took me aside and said, "You are Rob Lee, and need to be Rob Lee. You can't be Janie Bowman, and you can't walk like Janie Bowman. So quit limping."

"No!" I shouted back.

"Yes," she said, gently but firmly. She wasn't about to be intimidated by a petulant child. "Walk like Rob Lee. Be yourself."

Sure enough, when my parents returned from work, the limp was gone. They were thrilled and thanked Janie for her help. But my desire to incorporate Janie into every part of my life remained.

We spent much of our time together in our tiny, wood-paneled kitchen. At midday, Janie would sit me down at the little wooden table just off the kitchen and prepare me lunch. I can still smell the meat cooking, and see her sitting down next to me to help cut up my food. In the evenings, my family would sit at that same table and we'd eat our dinner together, but at lunchtime, I noticed that this was not the case. While Janie would sit next to me, she would never, ever eat alongside me. If I were lucky enough to have pizza, Janie would never indulge. When she cooked sausage, I would finish eating and she would clear my plate to the sink. I ate alone.

Then, after I finished eating, Janie would take out a plate, some utensils, and a drinking glass from a bag she'd brought from home. She then would prepare her own food and eat it quickly while keeping an eye on me from across the room.

Even as a young child, Janie's behavior bewildered me. Why wouldn't she eat with me, like my parents did? Why did she bring her own forks and knives and plates when there were plenty in our house? One afternoon as I was eating lunch, I decided to ask. The story has been recounted by my parents many times over the years.

"Why won't you eat with me?" I asked.

"It's your turn to eat lunch," Janie said, continuing to cut up the sausage she had cooked for me. "When you're finished, I'll eat the lunch I brought for myself. Now eat up."

"But why?"

"Because you're you, and I'm me," she said. "Just like you have to walk like you and I walk like me, you eat at your time and I eat at mine. We're just different."

"We're not different!" I screamed at her, my shrill child's voice reverberating through the house.

Janie was taken aback, slouching down into the kitchen chair. She said nothing else, but the look of anguish on her face said enough. My mind raced. Somehow, I had hurt the woman who meant so much to me. She was upset with me. I began to cry.

"This is just how things are," she said, trying to calm me down. "It's not good or bad, it's just how they are. You'll learn. Now come on, eat your lunch."

The rest of that day is a blur, lost to time. It would take years for me to understand what was really going on, to see that the culture of the Jim Crow South still persists to this day, forming an unjust and unholy barrier between white people and black people. It was a barrier that Janie never quite crossed, even when she prayed with me, rocked me in her arms, or prepared lunch for me. I don't know what Janie was thinking that day—and I won't try to guess. Her feelings and her voice are hers and hers alone. But the subtext of her pointing out our differences was clear. This caring, accomplished black woman would not use the utensils of a white family, or sit down with them to eat— even with a child. And especially not a child named Robert Lee. This barrier, sadly, kept me from knowing Janie more fully.

Shortly before I entered preschool, Janie was diagnosed with cancer. With her immune system compromised from the treatment, her doctors told her it would be best if she didn't interact with children, who are prone to colds and bugs and other illnesses. She just shouldn't risk it, they told her. But Janie continued to care for me, even refusing to wear the latex gloves that as a former nurse, she knew would better protect her. She didn't want there to be any more of a barrier between us. She was that kind of person.

ONE THING I'VE learned recently as I've crisscrossed the country, talking with and listening to racial justice advocates, is that the starting point for racial reconciliation must include the recognition that many of us, especially white people, come from a place of privilege.

But for many white people, the idea of being privileged seems like nonsense. About 40 percent of food stamp recipients are white, and many live in crushing poverty. So it's no surprise that some white people recoil when told that their skin color gives them privileges not afforded to other races. If it hasn't helped them become economically secure, the thinking goes, it probably hasn't helped with anything else.

Being poor in the South is no picnic, black or white. Indicators show that as a region, we lag behind the rest of the country in health, education, and overall quality of life. That being said, it is much easier to navigate the South when you are white. All white people benefit from the systemic acts of racism at play in the policies of our government. Laws about where people could buy homes kept blacks and whites segregated up until the late twentieth century, with black people getting the short end of the stick time and again. Drug laws have unfairly targeted people of color, leading to overrepresentation of black men in our nation's vast prison network. Once they are released, other laws make it difficult for them to find meaningful employment, and the cycle of discrimination continues.

As social justice activist Rev. Dr. William Barber II says, "When talking about the statues, we can't forget about the statutes." These carefully laid systems have ensured that persons of color in this nation have never been dealt a fair hand. This will only continue until people recognize the privileges afforded to Southern white people, and then set out to change them.

Looking back on that day in the kitchen, I see how although I didn't mean any harm to Janie, the dynamics of our relationship were such that I couldn't change anything by shouting over the chasm of race that divided us. At the end of the day, I was yet another white person—albeit a young one—telling her how to behave.

Years later, when I was in high school, I decided to seek out Janie. I had been contemplating a call to ministry and I wanted this woman to know what an impact she had had on my faith life. Even though she had proclaimed we were different years ago, I wanted to show her that I was in this for the long haul and committed to working for change.

I walked up to Janie's brick house with my dad and pressed the doorbell. I was a bit nervous about how our conversation would go, but excited to fill her in on the news.

The door opened and a woman asked if she could help us.

"I'm Rob Lee. Is Janie home?"

"Nope, she's not here," the woman replied matter-of-factly, "She died a few years ago."

"Oh," I said. "She used to take care of me, and I wanted to share some good news with her."

"Sorry, can't help you. Have a good day."

That was it. There wouldn't be a reunion for us. The one person who could fill me in on what happened all those years ago was gone. I was left with my memory of the event, my parents' retelling of it, and lots and lots of questions that would remain unanswered. Having pumped myself up for this meeting with Janie, I felt so deflated. I cried as my father and I walked to the car and made our way home.

Janie Bowman changed my life for the better, loving me in a way that few other people could. I regret that we lost touch before I could tell her how much she meant to me.

Now that I'm a bit older, the optics of my time with Janie are coming into focus. A hardworking and relatively well-off white couple hiring a black woman to care for their son seems, well, antiquated. And while I don't mean to accuse my parents of supporting racist structures still common in the South, I recognize the optics aren't the best.

I do know that however common, this experience, sadly, often fails to translate into understanding between white men and black women. Why would it? The institutional and societal challenges to racial reconciliation are often stronger than even the closest individual relationships. Several of my peers and family members were raised in situations similar to mine, with black women caring for them as children, yet today they wouldn't think twice before telling a racist joke or expressing a racist viewpoint. I suspect that the power dynamics of the relationship between white parents and black caregivers are structured in a way that feeds this unhealthy dynamic.

But I can't help but think there was something bigger

at work here than my parents, Janie, and me. Had it not been for Janie, who taught me that differences are real but shouldn't be divisive, I might have simply continued along with the flow of my surrounding culture. For many, the pull is just too strong to resist. But Janie and my parents set me on a path to understand that we aren't bound by cultural norms, that we have the freedom to resist and chart a new course.

Back in the 1970s, my parents had been part of Statesville's attempts at school integration. They told me repeatedly how important it is for white and black students to learn together. Later on, my mom worked on the team at Iredell Memorial who cared for the hospital's first HIV/AIDS patient, who happened to be African American. Mom told me how important it was for both black and white patients to be treated with respect and dignity. Moments like these were instrumental in helping me see racism for the sin it is.

My parents aren't theologians or ministers, but the lessons they taught me hold deep theological truths, even if they were not expressed to me that way. It seems to me that there has always been a hint of liberation within the faith tradition I claim. From Abraham going from a country where he was comfortable to the great unknown that God had promised him, to Moses leading the people through the sea out of Egypt, to the kings and prophets and on to Jesus and his apostles and disciples, all have woven a tapestry saying that the way things are isn't the way things have to be. Had it not been for the saints in my life contained within the pages of this memoir, I might have never received the faith that would lead to the liberating theology I now know.

In the critically acclaimed film *The Help,* there's a scene in which the maid, played by Viola Davis, looks at her socialite boss and says, "Ain't you tired, Miss Hilly?" The whole of Creation groans, as we read in Paul's Letter to the Romans, under the weight of sin—and, I believe, under the sin of racism. It's a sin that we have enacted through chattel slavery and the slave trade, through the half-hearted efforts of the failed Reconstruction, to the evil of the Jim Crow era and the Confederate monuments that still stand today. Our nation, our world, is tired.

But the night of weeping doesn't have to last forever. Just as Janie knew that the sweet hour of prayer was longer than one hour on Sunday morning, we, too, must believe that we are inextricably connected in the South and beyond, and that we have an obligation to take seriously how our actions affect one another.

As I write this, it is the eve of the anniversary of my baptism, All Saints' Day, in which the Protestant tradition remembers those who have gone before us, those who have completed the marathon and race of life. It is my fervent prayer that Janie can peer beyond the veil and see the pages of this book. If she can, I hope she is proud. I hope she knows I am working for a better and more just society. Finally, I hope in the hereafter, as much as one can hope for such things, that she has been fully and completely restored to the original glory God intended for her, free from cancer and free from the disease we know on earth as the Jim Crow South. It was my honor to learn from her the value of what Paul said in his letter to the Galatians, "There is no longer Jew or Greek, there is no longer slave or free, there is no longer male or female; for all of you are one in Christ Jesus."

5

In the South the war is what A.D. is elsewhere:
They date from it.

—MARK TWAIN, *LIFE ON THE MISSISSIPPI*

IN THE SOUTH, we're taught that racism is a sad fact of our past, part of the "Old South" that is being replaced by a "post-racial society" in which people are judged by the content of their character and not by the color of their skin. But my experience growing up shows this is not the case. Racism is a part of childhood in the South, no matter how hard we work to cover it with a coat of paint. Whether it was the kids at my all-white Christian day school who made jokes about black people that they no doubt learned around their kitchen tables, or the way our town was split along racial lines, the divide between blacks and whites saturates communities like Statesville. This latent racism, which is inescapable whether or not one chooses to acknowledge it, first became evident to me at the age of six, when my parents took my brother and me to a local Civil War reenactment.

Allison Woods is a giant piece of land twenty minutes outside downtown Statesville. The stretch of grass once served as an airstrip, but today it plays home to a number of events, including celebrations, hikes, and, most notably, the war reenactments that are commonplace in the South. Statesville's most famous battle dates back to the French and Indian War in the mid-eighteenth century. I remember watching those reenactments as a child, excited to see the costumes, listen to the sound of gunshots, and learn a little history at the same time. It was as though that painting in my Nana's living room had come to life, right before my eyes. Having seen how much my brother and I enjoyed these events, my parents decided to take us to a Civil War reenactment when they found out one was happening close to home.

It was summer, and the humid air suggested that a thunderstorm or downpour wasn't far off. As we took our place on a green knoll above the field and waited for the battle to begin, I looked around and saw that the surrounding crowd was made up of people just like us, white and Southern, though it skewed a bit older than our young family. I remember seeing Confederate flags everywhere. Not just on the battlefield and in the officers' tents, but also on the bumpers of cars in the parking area and on the T-shirts worn by some of the spectators. I recognized some of the folks I would see around town, both seated among the crowd and also donning costumes for the battle.

Suddenly the contest began. Two formations appeared on opposite sides of the field. Men in gray wool uniforms, carrying the flag of the Commonwealth of Virginia, represented the Confederate side. On the Union side stood men in blue wool uniforms, carrying the banner of the United States from that time, with thirty-five stars and thirteen stripes. The rifles, cannons, and horses provided plenty of entertainment for my brother and me, who were taken in by the spectacle of men shooting at one another, some appearing to fall dead on the field right in front of us. The formations were so historically accurate, we were told, General Lee would have felt right at home had he been transported to this very spot.

To their credit, the organizers interspersed within all the action several lessons of history, which I took in with delight. They explained how the rifles worked, the challenges of moving cannons across muddy battlefields, and how disease would often kill more men than the bullets flying at them.

Even the most devoted Civil War reenactors need a break from the humidity, so after a few hours of fighting, the men retreated to their tents. My father knelt down to my brother and me and offered us what then seemed like the chance of a lifetime.

"Would you two like to meet some of the officers?"

We didn't hesitate.

"Yes!" we screamed in unison.

My dad happened to know the guy who ran some of the events at Allison Woods, and this friend had invited us to visit the leaders' tents. Situated at either end of the battlefield, the actors from the North and the South each had tents where they donned their costumes, went over battle plans, and grabbed a beer or two in between sets. We headed, of course, to the tent where the actors in gray had assembled. Even if my parents were uncomfortable with some aspects of life in the South, it only made sense that we would root for "our side."

We walked into what was essentially a party, the sounds of beer cans being popped open and uproarious laughter at not-so-appropriate jokes. Some of the faces I recognized from church; others were new to me. Most of the actors were older, all were white, and many of them hadn't noticed that two children had come inside. My parents made small talk with some of the folks they recognized from town as my brother and I gawked at the uniforms, guns, and cannons.

Off in the distance, out of our earshot, were some actors who were black—there to represent the black soldiers, some of them former slaves, who fought valiantly for the North. In recent years, especially, African Americans with an interest in history have made strides in ensuring the stories of these heroes aren't being overlooked. But as the white men in the tent carried on, I started hearing words that even as a six-year-old I knew were not polite. "Colored people." "N—." The look on my parents' faces—quick, uncomfortable glances to each other—confirmed that they were not nice things.

I don't remember why the men were using those words to describe their fellow reenactment enthusiasts. Some black leaders in Statesville had expressed opposition to the reenactment; perhaps they were talking about that. It's possible, too, that the white men didn't even think they were being particularly hateful. It doesn't change how wrong it was for them to utter such words.

I cringe writing those words today, but the sad fact is that it remains fairly unremarkable to hear them in Statesville. I heard them in school, in other people's homes, and even at my own family gatherings. I remember my great-grandmother, whom we called Super Granny, had done secretary work for a man who was a member of the local chapter of the Ku Klux Klan. I don't know how Super Granny felt about her boss being a member of the Klan, as she died before I was old enough to ask such a question. But I do know that she used "colored people" and the N-word freely, no matter how many times my parents asked her to stop. For a certain generation of white Southerners, many of whom are still living, those were simply the words they used. The Klan still maintains an active presence near Statesville, holding an annual meeting in a local town called Love Valley, of all things. When I learned in high school that some people who live just down the street from me were known to attend this meeting, it sent a wave of sadness through me.

On that day in the tent, twenty years ago, my parents quickly wrapped up their conversations, and on the way out, my dad thanked his host for the invitation to visit.

In the minivan on the ride home, my mom navigated a difficult but necessary conversation with Scott and me about what we had just seen and heard.

"Why did those people say those things?" I asked hesitantly.

"Because they are filled with hate," she said quickly, clearly still bothered by what we'd heard.

"Those words are never appropriate," she continued. "They mean something hateful. Some people would be hurt if they overheard them. We don't use them, okay?"

"Okay," we said.

But she wasn't finished.

"It isn't just an issue of manners," she said. "They're never appropriate to use, even if there's nobody around who might be hurt by them."

My mother used the experience in the tent as a theological reflection on the dignity of all people. She repeated to us the lessons we learned in church, that all people are created in God's image and that we all deserve respect because of that fact alone. Nothing else mattered—not how someone looked, how much money someone had, and especially not the color of someone's skin. Those words we heard in the tent, even if they were said with a sense of levity that suggested humor, were words that rejected God's love.

MY AIM IN this is not to present Statesville as a racist cesspool whose residents are stuck in the nineteenth century. Mixed in with stories like this one is a lot of real beauty—and Statesville remains a pleasant place for many of its residents. Our parks are lush and green, resplendent with tulips and flowering trees in spring. In true Southern fashion, people are friendly, and small talk remains an activity that they genuinely enjoy—something to savor, not blow past.

There's still a real sense of community here, with the town rallying around the high school in football season and engaging with their churches for social and charity events. That's why my wife and I have decided to settle down here. We recently bought a home in Statesville and, in the process, are making a long-term commitment to this community that has so much good in it. Stephanie and I desperately want all residents of our community to feel the welcome we feel.

Sometimes, I must admit, it's hard not to look back at my history in this place without rose-tinted glasses. For instance, growing up, a highlight of each summer was going out to the Fort Dobbs State Historic Site for the hospital picnic, a sort of mini-carnival that, looking back, brought out the best of Statesville. By that point, my mom was a hospital director, but rank was irrelevant during the picnic. The former president of the hospital, Arnold Nunnery, was on hand to chat with the families of the workers who made the hospital run. At the time, Fort Dobbs was a giant grassy crater, not unlike the pit from *Parks and Rec*. But the bounce house, kid-sized train, and seemingly endless supply of barbecue transformed the hollow into an amusement park that we loved unabashedly. The point of the picnic was simply to provide a chance for the staff and their families to bond outside of work, an opportunity to get to know neighbors and friends in a deeper way.

Then there were the organized activities, many of which were centered around faith. Take the Boy Scouts, as another example. Like many boys growing up in the South, I spent a great deal of time involved with my local Boy Scout troop. The one I joined was affiliated with a large Baptist church, an evangelical congregation that some people jokingly refer to as the Liberty University of Statesville—meaning that it's unabashedly conservative, championing so-called traditional values and proud of its fervent patriotism. For most of my time in the Scouts, politics was far from my mind. Instead, we focused on learning how to tie knots, make crafts, survive in the wilderness, and live as good citizens.

As I grew older and decided to seek the rank of Eagle

Scout, I wanted to take on a community service project that would give something back to my community. I thought of all the time my friends and family and I had spent at Fort Dobbs—which was still more or less a giant grassy pit—and decided I'd try to make improvements in some small way.

After talking with my family and some of the other Scouts, I decided I would raise funds to build a fence along a quarter-mile perimeter of Fort Dobbs. A long-term goal of the people who managed the historical site was to make it look exactly as it did during the French and Indian War. They noted that there would have been a fence around the site back in the eighteenth century, but there wasn't one today. So I decided to undertake this particular part of restoration. We estimated that we'd need about $4,500 to buy materials for a fence made of locust wood, a hard, splintery lumber often associated with the mountains of North Carolina. I called and wrote letters to the Friends of Fort Dobbs asking for donations. Then I solicited donations from friends, family members, and community leaders. I was blown away by the response. Together, residents of Statesville pooled more than enough for the materials. Instead of the $4,500 I budgeted for the project, we raised close to $6,000. This meant we could cover the transit cost and even provide lunch to the twenty or so volunteers who agreed to help assemble the rail-style fence.

Finally, construction day arrived. On a warm Friday morning, a large red truck pulled up to Fort Dobbs,

packed with pallets of locust wood. Putting our lemon-
ade aside and grabbing our work gloves, we unloaded the
wood and got to work. The crew included members of my
family and my entire Scout troop. It was like assembling a
giant puzzle, fitting together the A-frame–style fence piece
by piece. It was slow going, and I wondered if we'd actually
finish the project in time. But after a break for Chick-fil-A
sandwiches, the quintessential Southern lunch on a day
like that, and some griping about the heat, we got back
to work. By the time the sun went down, Fort Dobbs had
a new fence—and I had a renewed faith in the people of
Statesville.

As with everything in Statesville, my time in the Scouts
was more complicated than it seemed on the surface. I
would celebrate years later when a few of my fellow Scouts
came out as gay, but it pained me to remember the ho-
mophobia rampant among Scout leaders, with hurtful
words coming even from the boys' own fathers. On one
rafting trip, a fellow Scout confided in me that he was
gay, and he hadn't had the courage to tell many people.
I thanked him for trusting me and told him everything
would be okay, and not to worry. But I was wrong.

Later on during that trip, one of the volunteers, a father
of one of the Scouts, told some of the kids to "stop being
so gay." I glanced with horror at my friend, who looked
painfully away. I didn't know what to do. Luckily I didn't
have to do much.

"Cut that out," my dad said. "So what if they are?"

I was in awe of my father, who was able to muster up the courage to take on some of his peers over an issue that certainly would've been awkward around a group of teenage boys. In fact, that very troop eventually disbanded over the question of gay Scouts, another sad reminder of how much further Statesville has to go. Deep down, I suspect that many of the homophobic scoutmasters wanted to be accepting, but it was just too tough a road to walk with the climate of the time and the way their conservative church treated the LGBTQ community.

There is a perception among some that people in the South are backward, that we're a bunch of racist hicks clinging to guns and fundamentalist Christianity, out of touch with the modern world. This isn't the case, at least not always, and it's not my aim to contribute to this stereotype. I want people to see that there is goodness and beauty in our culture and kindness in our faith. Racism has permeated all of it, and our culture at large has yet to reckon with this ugly stain. But deep in the Blue Ridge Mountains, in the red clay of the Piedmont—some of the most beautiful natural landscapes on earth—are good people not content with the status quo. Each time they speak up, like my dad did on that day, it creates a new possibility for someone else to follow in their steps.

IT WOULD BE easy to gloss over the ugliness of coming of age in this place that prides itself on progress. Many people do, willfully turning a blind eye to the systems and structures that benefit one group of people at the expense of another. But when my wife and I decided that we'd settle down in Statesville, we did so with eyes wide open to the challenges that remain today, challenges that I pray our future children will not look on idly. A recent example captures the work that remains.

Before my wife and I moved back to Statesville, we occasionally made our way there to visit family and attend our childhood church. We were gathered in the sanctuary one Sunday talking about the church's various social ministries for the poor and marginalized communities in town. The conversation was lively and energetic, even if the task in front of us felt daunting. Then a longtime member of the church spoke up.

"We've got to help the colored people, too," she said.

I gently but firmly pushed back.

"You can't talk like that," I said, with a note of pleading and perhaps sheepishness in my voice. But before I could explain why, I saw that other members of the church were staring at me, their eyes big with disbelief. My cheeks burned red. They looked shocked that I would talk back to an older, more respected member of the church. She was only trying to help, after all. After a short period of silence, the group went on with the agenda, paying no attention to my interruption.

When I returned home that night, I told my mom what had happened at the church. I told her how I had admonished the woman, however gently, only to be made to feel as if I were the one who had said something offensive. Racism in Statesville is so pervasive, even well-meaning people can't hear it when it flows from their own mouths.

"Is this the new normal?" I asked my mom, thinking that maybe the wave of white nationalism unleashed after the election of President Trump had infiltrated my hometown, with a whopping 67 percent voting for him.

"This is the way it's always been," she said. "This has always been normal."

This is Statesville, after all, a place where the local barbershop once hosted a raffle fundraiser for a family dealing with cancer, and the winner received a new AR-15 rifle—the same style of gun that was used to murder children in a Connecticut school, worshippers at a Texas church, and students at a high school in Parkland, Florida. Even in our charitable acts, the culture of violence, from race to weapons, runs deep here.

I sighed.

"I don't know, Mom, things need to change. How can we live in a place like this?" I asked her.

She thought for a moment, aware of my anger and

perhaps wanting to encourage me not to give up just yet on Statesville.

"Well, try to be patient," my mom told me. "You know everyone has a unique journey to take. Pray for hers. That's how things will change."

"Will that ever be enough—will that prayer ever work?" I asked.

My mom, with her ever-sensitive empathy, looked at me, hugged me tight, then looked at Stephanie and said, "I hope you know we'd be bailing you out of jail if you were a child of the sixties—and I would do it now, too— but remember this journey is so difficult for so many, and we must work for the day of our Lord Jesus Christ." Although a nurse, my mom has always been something of a preacher.

It was then I realized what she meant. Prayer isn't passive. It is an active and integral part of my mom's faith and her wish for change in our part of the country. In the vein of Abraham Heschel she believes that prayer sometimes requires "praying with your feet." And though at times she has been frustrated with my clunky way of forcing change, I know she is proud and wants the same change I yearn for. That is, after all, how she raised me.

6

I wish I knew how it would feel to be free.

—NINA SIMONE

T HE BATTLE FLAG of the Army of Northern Virginia, with a red square cut in fours by two blue bars and a number of white stars, is a common sight around Statesville and much of the South. Perversely, some describe it as "the Southern cross," which shows just how easily white Christianity has mingled with white supremacy. But there is one Confederate flag, in particular, that still haunts me. *That* flag was the one I bought during a family excursion to Arlington House.

Situated high atop a hill in Arlington National Cemetery, directly across the Potomac from the Lincoln Memorial, is the estate that once belonged to the family of General Robert E. Lee. According to the National Park Service, which maintains the house as part of the Robert E. Lee Memorial, the house is meant to highlight Lee's "role in promoting peace and reunion after the Civil War" and move visitors to contemplate "some of the most difficult aspects of American history: military service; sacrifice; citizenship; duty; loyalty; slavery and freedom." It was here that Lee raised his seven children with his wife, Mary, and ran a plantation belonging to his father-in-law.

According to his sympathetic biographers, Lee sharpened his skills as a successful administrator at Arlington House by making the plantation more efficient and profitable. Like so much of Lee's mythology, that is a sanitized and sugarcoated piece of history. What Lee actually did at Arlington House was use human beings enslaved by the family—two hundred of them—in order to increase his family's wealth and prestige.

The Lees fled Arlington House early in the Civil War, and the property became a prime target for Union forces. Union troops were buried close to the house's foundation. Mary's prized rose garden was dug up and turned into another burial plot. Today, the grounds are home to Arlington National Cemetery, which is not a coincidence. The message from Union occupiers was clear: Betray the United States and face consequences. The Lees' beloved homestead was no longer their own.

Many summers during my childhood, my family would pile into our gray Chevy Tahoe and make the pilgrimage to Washington, D.C., for a visit to our ancestor's home. As a young kid, the place's history was not at the forefront of my mind. Instead, Arlington House was simply another interesting historical site to visit in a city teeming with them. Of course, the excitement of these visits was amplified by the fact that we were related to the man who once lived in that majestic place.

For a long time, I was proud to be an indirect descendant of Lee, fascinated that my family's ancestors had made an impact on our country and its history. Back home in North Carolina, any time I saw an image of Lee, I took pride in knowing that I was related to someone important enough to have a statue or painting created in his honor. Most of my friends couldn't claim having such a famous relative. Here we were, in my great-great-great-great uncle's house! Everywhere I looked, the "Lee" name was prominent, and I could claim some ownership over it.

"Man, it'd be nice if this place still belonged to the family," my Nana joked.

We laughed, comparing the opulence of the place to our nice but relatively modest houses back in Statesville. I see now, years later, how comments like this, however innocuous they felt, contribute to our culture's penchant for glossing over its painful past.

Like all good Southern boys, my brother and I loved playing war, using toy guns to imagine we were participants in the War of Northern Aggression, as our schoolteachers often called it. Later on, when I married a girl from Grafton, Massachusetts, a bedroom community outside

Boston, we exchanged stories about what it was like to be raised in places steeped in history. Children up north, I learned, read year after year about the Revolutionary War, basking in a time when the American ideals of freedom and liberty triumphed against British tyranny. It makes sense. Those battles took place not far from where they lived, and many of the ideals espoused by America's founders are still relevant today. Back home in Statesville, however, our history lessons seemed stuck in the nineteenth century, the valor of Southern generals fighting valiantly for states' rights taking precedence over all else. The ideas we read in those textbooks were supplemented with visits to Confederate battlefields dedicated to Confederate heroes, and visits to Arlington House.

The rooms of the house still contain articles of clothing and other items that belonged to Lee. I remember standing there, looking up at the ceiling where Lee's footsteps were heard as he paced up and down his study, struggling with his momentous decision. In that place where history was made, my fascination with Lee was awakened, just like it was when I looked at the painting on my grandmother's wall.

Before leaving after one visit, we walked by the gift shop, situated near the old slave quarters—rooms that were once home to the horrors of human bondage. Still riding high from the tour, I asked my mom to buy me a postcard of Lee from the gift shop. Though my family was ready to move on to other things, I wanted proof I had made my pilgrimage to the holy grounds of the Lee homestead.

"How about this flag, too?" I asked.

Flustered by trying to wrangle two young boys, a husband, and a mother-in-law into the car for the next stop on our trip, my mom took the flag, threw it on the counter with the rest of the souvenirs, and handed it all to the clerk for checkout. She paid, handed the bag to me, and we were on our way.

When we returned home, my mom took the postcard to get framed, and my dad helped me hang the flag above my twin bed, nestled between two large eagles printed on the wallpaper. I placed Lee's portrait postcard next to the flag, a fitting place, in my mind, for my namesake. Surveying the room, I felt a sense of pride in being connected to our family's past. It was as if I was doing something noble, taking time to learn about history and my ancestor's role in it.

I failed to realize at the time that these decorating decisions said something ugly about my heritage—and that shames me today. A few years later, as I prepared for the sacrament of confirmation, a beloved family friend would challenge me and help me realize the power that flag holds over too many people.

WHENEVER I VISITED my mom at work, her colleague and executive assistant Mrs. Bertha Hamilton always captivated me. She was a quiet woman, usually keeping to herself as she hummed a hymn and went on about her day. But her deep faithfulness drew me in. I peppered her with questions, usually trivial, and she would listen patiently before answering. But on the rare occasions when she made it clear that she had something to say, I listened up. (One thing Southern boys learn early on is that you listen when an elder is speaking.)

Our visits weren't particularly long—usually I'd just run up to my mom's office and give a quick hug to Mrs. Bertha before we left for home. But those interactions added up. As I prepared for confirmation at age thirteen, I knew immediately who I would ask to sponsor my initiation into the church.

Confirmation at Broad Street Methodist Church was in some ways formulaic. Each spring, a group of teenagers from the congregation selected mentors from the church community and met a number of times with them to discuss what it means to be an adult Christian. After a few months of these meetings, the confirmation class and the sponsors would gather inside the sanctuary for a laying-of-hands ceremony that sealed us with the gifts of the Holy Spirit as we transitioned into adult members of the Methodist Church.

Even as a teenager, I felt a spark, a sense that a calling

to religious life might be in store for me. Perhaps that's why some of the older members of the church invited me to preach at a special service planned by the teenagers at Broad Street. As the day approached, I asked my mom for ideas.

"Do what you need to do to get people to understand God's love for them," she suggested.

Easy enough.

I picked out a pair of crisp khakis, a white shirt, and a navy blue blazer. I asked if I could wear one of the robes favored by preachers at Broad Street, but was told, "No. Not yet."

The place was packed, filled with much of the usual congregation and more than a few young people who didn't normally make it in time for Sunday morning services. I started up to the pulpit, the same one I had come to admire from my time at church on Sunday mornings, and tried to take some deep breaths to calm myself down.

"God loves you," I said, as confidently and as convincingly as a thirteen-year-old first-time preacher can proclaim. "And we have to respond by marking the box 'yes' or 'no.'"

The point I was trying to get across was that God's love for us is infinite, unconditional, and ever present. It's up to us to decide how to respond to that love. If we accept God's love and love God in return, it will surely affect how we treat one another. After all, it's Jesus who tells us to love one another as God loves us.

I'm not sure I charted any new theological territory that night, but a number of people came up to me afterward and thanked me. A few even suggested I consider becoming a preacher. One woman, a greeter at our local Walmart, said decisively, "You're going to be a minister. And you're going to preach at my funeral!" I smiled awkwardly.

How did these people know I had been thinking about a life in ministry when I hadn't told anyone? Maybe it was time to explore the idea with someone else. And I knew just who I'd tell.

When I told the confirmation organizers that I had selected Mrs. Bertha as my sponsor, they were confused. Mrs. Bertha wasn't a member of our church community. She wasn't even United Methodist. But Mrs. Bertha was one of the only people I'd told about my sense that God might be calling me to ministry. She encouraged me to listen to that call. There was no one more important to the development of my faith than Mrs. Bertha, and I was convinced she should be the one to accompany me on this journey. Those in charge of the program came around.

I was excited to ask Mrs. Bertha, who by this point felt like a second grandmother to me. She had experienced many challenges during her life, both when she lived in New York City and then later on in Statesville. But she exuded a calming joy and an infectious sense of gratitude. I knew she was the right person for the job. So one afternoon at the hospital, I reminded her of the constant refrain given by Mom and Dad that she meant so much to my family.

"Mrs. Bertha, I'd be honored if you would be my confirmation sponsor; I need your help and your wisdom in this," I told her, a little embarrassed by such a sincere request.

"Oh, Rob, I'd love that!" she shot back, a big smile on both our faces.

Our first meeting took place at Mrs. Bertha's place of worship, Clark's Chapel Baptist Church. She had invited me to attend a service and said we could talk afterward. I entered the building excited—if a bit nervous. This was my first visit to a predominantly black church, and I wasn't sure what to expect. I was confident, however, that the worship experience would be different from the stuffy, albeit beautiful, mainline Protestant services I was used to.

The environment inside was electric. The people of that church celebrated their faith with an energy and a zeal that was simultaneously foreign and welcoming. Clark's Chapel had spent years raising money for a new sanctuary, and the people of the congregation beamed as they showed me their purple-carpeted sanctuary with white pews. Every member of the church was involved in worship in some way, whether through leading the service or reading from the Bible or singing in the choir or even hollering "Amen!" from the pews. The celebration was robust and fresh, and it showed me a side of the African American experience I had not encountered, even though it took place every Sunday morning just a short ride from my home. They sang many of the hymns that I knew, but in ways I had never heard before. Years later, with a seminary education under my belt, I realized that this has been a key feature of the African American church experience: taking a religion of slaveholders and making it the hope of the enslaved.

Following the service, Mrs. Bertha and I headed downstairs, with the discussion workbook from my church in hand. We fulfilled the church's requirements and checked off the topics we were told to discuss, like Methodist polity, history, and faith formation. Years later I still feel that Wesleyan formation in my bones. But then we moved on to the more current, and potentially more hazardous, issues of faith, war, poverty, politics—and race. Even then, I realized the scene was remarkable. A black woman spending part of her day in the basement of a black church teaching a white nephew of Robert E. Lee about Christian charity. Like many of my encounters with Mrs. Bertha, moments like this were possible only because of God's grace. I did my best to make them count, as we repeated these meetings several more times, usually in the fellowship hall back at Broad Street Methodist Church.

During one of these meetings, we talked about the Civil War. This was hardly unique. I was interested in politics and history, and Mrs. Bertha seemed to know so much about things I hadn't heard of in school or at home. I inundated her with questions, and she listened patiently as I tried to find the words to ask what was on my mind. But in this meeting, it was a question from Mrs. Bertha that led to a major turning point in my life, and in my understanding of my family legacy.

"So, tell me more about that visit to Arlington House," Mrs. Bertha said, picking up on a story I had told her about my family's summer trips. It had been a few years since the last visit to Arlington House, but I recounted the trip up with my family, told her about the visit to the gift shop, including the purchase of the flag and the photo of Lee.

"Where are they now?" she asked.

"Well, they're both hanging up in my room," I told her, reluctantly, sensing that something was wrong. "The flag's above my bed and the postcard nearby."

She sensed my discomfort, so she took her time. Her mouth grew tight as she sat there thinking.

"Oh, honey, why?" she finally asked.

"Well, he's my ancestor," I said in reply, though the pride I once felt in giving that answer had begun to dissipate.

Mrs. Bertha sat back in her folding chair and put her hand on her face as she thought about what to say next.

"You gotta take that down," she said. "You mean more to this world than this flag, and you've got to take that down."

By that point, I knew the flag was controversial from

the news stories that we'd talk about in class and the seg-
ments I saw on television. But it's also an undeniable part
of life in the South, especially on the north side of Statesville where I lived. When I thought of the people I knew
who displayed the flag on their lawns or walls, I thought
of people who were proud of their Southern heritage. I
myself had it hanging up in my room, and I didn't think
I was racist. My parents knew it was there, and I didn't
think they were racist, either. It was simply an expression
of our Southern culture. What was wrong with that? Un-
convinced as to why I should remove it, I asked Mrs. Bertha to explain.

She told me in painful detail how the Confederacy
viewed black people, how it thrived on an institution that
dehumanized men, women, and children, enslaved them
and exploited them for profit. She talked about how even
after the South fell, laws were put in place to ensure that
black Americans would never be equal with whites. I still
remember her telling me that, contrary to the narrative in
my history books from school, Reconstruction had failed
and the flag became a symbol of that retrenchment. She
explained how even today, the effects of slavery are still all
too evident, how racial reconciliation is still a goal to be
pursued and not a victory to be celebrated.

As I sat there listening, I burned red with shame and
confusion. I had known some of the history of the flag, but
I'd never suspected it could still hurt someone today. It was

history, after all. Still, I knew full well that the flag didn't fly on the south side of Statesville, where Mrs. Bertha and people like her lived. That I couldn't draw the obvious conclusion from that on my own—that the flag is a sign of *white* Southern culture—embarrassed me. Mrs. Bertha was right. The flag had to go.

My dad picked me up from the church and we drove home in silence. I couldn't stop thinking about what Mrs. Bertha had told me to do. When we got home, I went straight to my bedroom, turned on the light, and walked over to the postcard of General Lee. I removed the photo from the wall, placed it inside a small drawer on my bedside table, and took out the thumbtacks holding up the flag. I folded it up quickly and, still feeling shame, placed it inside the drawer, covering the postcard of Lee. I felt glad that I had followed through on my promise to Mrs. Bertha, but filled with regret that I hadn't done this sooner, on my own accord.

I didn't make a big deal of it afterward. I never told my parents I had decided to take the symbols down, and my friends who had Confederate paraphernalia in their own bedrooms never asked about it when they visited.

During our next meeting, I decided that Mrs. Bertha would be the only person I told.

"I did what you suggested," I told her sheepishly.

Before I could go into details—how I removed the pins, folded the flag, took down the postcard—or tell her how sorry I was, she cut me off. Her response was characteristic of her personality: warm, direct, and to the point.

"I knew you would" was all she said.

And then we moved on. That was that. She could have rubbed it in; she could have gone on about how ignorant I had been to display such symbols in the first place. She would have been justified, and that's certainly one way to teach a lesson. But we simply moved on to the next session in the confirmation book. The whole experience was a moment of grace and reconciliation, one that is possible only when two people encounter each other and are willing to confront difficult issues like race, history, and ancestry.

Michael Korda, in his biography of Lee, includes an observation about Lee and his legacy that's stuck with me: "As the Confederacy shrank, [Lee] grew, symbolizing the unshakable spirit of resistance, stubborn hope, courage, and honor—beyond criticism, perhaps even beyond reason." It's true. As the old ways of life in the South are rightfully challenged, people resistant to change cling ever tighter to Lee and what he represented. Those ideas are small, but in the minds of those who fear change, they grow ever bigger.

Several years after I took the Confederate flag down from my bedroom wall, I asked my mom what she and my dad had been thinking in letting me put it up in the first place. I've come to know my parents as Southerners who are proud of our home but who nonetheless resist the racial components here that are unjust toward African Americans and other minorities. That they would buy their middle school son a Confederate flag and let him hang it in his bedroom just doesn't square with what I know about them today. So I asked my mom, "What was that all about?"

She thought for a moment, as she always does before answering a question, and said, "I've always been uncomfortable with the Confederate flag," she said. But she and my dad had talked about it when I first expressed an interest in getting one, and decided that I should be allowed to make my own decisions, even if they thought some were mistakes.

"When you decided you wanted the flag, it was kind of painful for me," she told me. "It was uncomfortable for me."

Looking back, I wish my mom would have told me the flag made her hurt. Perhaps a stubborn teenage boy wouldn't have cared, but at least I would have known something was wrong with this piece of cloth and what it has come to represent.

"Now, of course, it didn't stay in your room very long," my mom added. "And you came to the realization that each time we saw it, we remembered what society had made of it."

She's right, I did come to that realization. But not on my own. And that's why I believe dialogue around these issues is so important today. If I hadn't sought out, and listened to, the opinions of someone different from me, maybe I would have kept it hanging up, the symbol seeping deeper and deeper into my being. But because Mrs. Bertha spoke up, because she offered grace, because she gifted me with knowledge of my own past in a hope for a better future, I had the consciousness to take it down.

IN NOVEMBER 2017, I visited Arlington House again. I wanted to be back in the space, to grapple once again with the history of my family and the history of our nation. As we walked the halls of Lee's house, I felt once again the history filtering through the cracks in the plaster and paint.

"Wasn't he nice to his slaves?" a white lady asked the black park ranger leading us through the house.

"It depends if you count enslavement as nice," the tour guide dryly replied.

The woman's question brings up a deep truth, namely, that it matters how we interpret history. Much of the South's history is ugly and unpleasant. For a family spending a day touring the majestic grounds of Arlington House, the temptation to gloss over some of that painful past is strong. Religion, politics, and money are verboten topics in some families. White people tend to add slavery and racism to that list. Those issues are too divisive, and besides, we tell ourselves, they are problems for other people to deal with. But ignorance is not bliss. If we ignore the violence from our past we are doomed to repeat it again in the future.

"Well, didn't he free his slaves at the onset of the war?" the same woman asked.

"Yes, but they were enslaved before that," the park ranger responded, emphasizing the word "enslaved" as if it should be obvious that no, Lee was not kind or nice or fair to his slaves. They were slaves!

I will never be able to scrub from my mind the images of those rooms where my distant uncle forced his slaves to work in the kitchen. I will never be able to forget that scene in my imagination. But I can work to make sure our history is remembered and try to give attention to what really matters: not the redemption of the Lee family name, but the reconciliation here in the South, and elsewhere, between people of all races.

At the gift shop in Arlington, I bought a bust of Robert E. Lee, similar to how my parents once bought something for me, but this time, it was different. One day, years from now, when Stephanie and I have kids, I will take this bust down from storage and tell them the story of our family lineage. I will tell them all of it, and I will hold nothing back.

7

As we let our own light shine, we unconsciously
give other people permission to do the same.
As we are liberated from our own fear,
our presence automatically liberates others.

—MARIANNE WILLIAMSON

MY LIFE CHANGED because of people like
Mother Aleen, Janie Bowman, and Mrs. Bertha
Hamilton, black women who tirelessly and selflessly invited me to consider another way of seeing our town and
the world. Without them, it's probable my outlook on issues of race and justice would mirror that of my peers.

I can't say for certain whether my friends in grade
school, and later in high school, bullied black students,
or even employed the kind of overt racism that has sadly
become more acceptable over the past couple of years. I
do know that they were certainly unwilling to confront
the stark challenges that remain in ushering in reconciliation. Just like the adults touring Arlington House, who
didn't want the truth of our complicated past to ruin a

perfectly good day, my classmates would rather not have sought to understand how their actions might contribute to the gulf that continues to separate us based on nothing but race. I'm sure of this because I've recently settled back in Statesville and have reconnected, however informally, with my classmates from my early days at a Southern Baptist Christian school in Statesville and some peers from the public high school I chose to attend when I got older.

My parents meant well in sending me to a fundamentalist Christian school from kindergarten to eighth grade, but I was miserable. As we progressed from grade to grade, we were taught scriptural interpretations that just didn't make sense to me, like when the teachers told us that the earth was just six thousand or so years old.

"But what about dinosaurs?" I wondered.

My family and I generally held more progressive views than my teachers, and I always felt like I was on the margins of the nearly all-white Christian school. My attitude came across as bratty to my teachers, who never warmed up to my continuous challenges and questions. Though my parents never discouraged my curiosity, I can't imagine it was easy for them to sit in parent-teacher conferences and listen to the sighs from my teachers.

Still, when it came time to choose where I'd attend high school, my parents assumed I would take the path of least resistance and finish my education at the Christian school. So when I told them that I wanted to check out the public high school, they were a bit taken aback.

"You know that it will be very different for you, right?" my mom asked, perhaps a bit nervous that an already awkward kid might feel even more out of place in the bigger, more racially diverse public high school. Though she and my dad had attended the same school years earlier, Statesville High wasn't the kind of place where a kid who lived in the country club usually went.

"I don't know what I'd be getting myself into," I admitted to her, "but I'd like to at least take a tour."

We agreed, and I headed to the large brick edifice in the center of town for a tour of what I hoped would be my new school. Immediately, I felt relief. The student body looked more like Statesville than it did in the halls of my Christian school. The staff, too, was more diverse, with a distinguished African American man serving as principal. I was tired of my status quo and I wanted something different. Mrs. Bertha, during one of our chats at the hospital, encouraged me to explore Statesville High. It would be different, she acknowledged, but it would do me good. That had sealed the deal.

The transition to public school wasn't easy to navigate. Even simple things, like lunch, proved to be a bit of a challenge at first. Lunches at my small Christian school were catered by local restaurants and brought to us by school staff. At Statesville High, like most big schools, we grabbed a tray, stood in line, chose our food, and then tried to find a seat with people we knew. The process was fairly horrifying for a newbie like me. Social situations have always stressed me out a little bit, and there's perhaps no more anxiety-inducing scene for an awkward-feeling young man than lunch in the cafeteria on the first day of school.

I didn't exactly thrive immediately. On my first day, I grabbed a tray and got my food just fine. But as I turned to go find a seat, I dropped the tray, its contents flying everywhere. I was mortified, expecting the worst. But no one pointed, no one laughed. Instead, a kind African American lunch lady called me over.

"Sweetie, don't worry about it. Grab yourself a new lunch," she said.

I emerged from my moment of panic mostly unscathed. What could have quickly spiraled into a nightmare—at least for an already nervous kid on his first day at a new school—instead turned into a small moment of God's grace. I tried to muster a smile.

"Thanks so much," I said, intent on conveying my gratitude for an act of kindness that, in that moment, felt like everything to me. But she had already moved on, smiling and laughing with the long line of kids behind me. Life goes on.

It only got better from there, though I had occasional doubts about whether I had made the right choice. While I had grown up around many older black people, and counted wise black women among those closest to me, I didn't have any black friends my age. When I walked into the band room for my first practice, I was, much to my surprise, very clearly in the minority. I wasn't scared, just a bit startled and nervous about being the new kid in another class where everyone seemed to know one another.

"What's your name?" one outgoing student asked me.

"Rob," I told him.

"Where are you from?" another student wanted to know. I told him.

"What was that like?" another asked when I told them about my old school, and why I was starting here not knowing anyone else.

Soon, we were all chatting, other kids were jumping in with their own stories, and I was just another student in the classroom. I would go on to flourish at Statesville High, never once regretting the decision to leave the narrowness of my Christian school behind.

A YEAR LATER, at the start of my sophomore year, I was selected to be a drum major in our high school marching band. The position works kind of like the captain of a football team, an opportunity to gain some leadership skills while assisting the adults in charge. By this point, the dynamic at Statesville High, especially around issues of race that I hadn't noticed on my first visit, were blazing and visible. The demarcations between black and white may not have been officially laid out, but they were there if you looked. Some things just never felt right, as if there were a code designed to keep the white students, a minority in the school, separated from the black students.

Why were the advanced placement classes filled with white students? How was it possible that in a school that was mostly black, white students could go most of the day surrounded by other students who looked just like them? Why did the parents of Statesville so vigorously support the notion of neighborhood schools? (Later, I would realize the neighborhoods were intensely segregated. By advocating for these schools, parents were ensuring segregation would continue unchallenged.)

When I asked around about why these things were, there were no easy answers, or at least none that satisfied me. "These are just how the classes were assigned," a teacher told me. "Focus on your work." Deep down, I suspected something bigger was going on. Though I didn't understand it fully then, the systemic racism that pervades much of Statesville was at play, even if the adults in charge wouldn't acknowledge it directly. Then there were the attitudes prevalent among some of my white peers.

IT WAS COMMON to hear black students at Statesville High use the N-word with one another, though often swapping out the -er for an -a at the end of it. This wasn't totally shocking, as the word has been reclaimed by some in the African American community as a way to deflate its power as a weapon of hate. The reality that young men would use it as they navigated the difficulties of figuring out adulthood was to be expected. But problems arose when some of my white peers also began using the word—sometimes even directing it at the black students. Beneath the patina of school spirit—Go Greyhounds!—a simmering racial tension animated much of our community. White people like me were missing the point.

Take the weekly football games, scenes taken right out of *Friday Night Lights*. It seemed that the entire town put everything on hold for a few hours and would head down to the Statesville High Stadium. Police would block off a stretch of road so that the marching band could make our way from the school to the stadium, the drum line keeping time and providing a burst of enthusiasm for the football team and their fans.

Once we got into the stadium, it was tradition for the hometown band to engage in a bit of teasing with the visiting team's band. When our rivals, North Iredell High, marched in, we'd play "Old McDonald" to greet them—a jab at their more rural, white community. When we visited North Iredell, they returned the favor by playing various rap songs that were popular at the time. The music was meant as a slur, a Southern insult meant to highlight that most of our school was African American. But many members of our band loved it. It was almost like being able to pick your own walk-on music before taking the plate.

Still, there was an ugly side to it all. North Iredell High, after all, was located near Love Valley, the town where the Klan meetings took place—and when we played there, the glares coming from some of the students and parents in the home bleachers showed me the song choice wasn't all in good fun. I felt a chill looking at those contorted faces, unsure why the venomous looks were so intense. Looking back, I'm not sure why I was surprised. After all, part of my duties as drum major was to keep our band members, many of whom were black, away from the home team's bleachers. Safety was paramount, especially after an ugly incident occurred that still shocks me today.

During an away game, deep in a part of the state where Klan meetings are still alive and well, our band was taking to the field for our halftime show. As the band members marched in step to their places, I hung back with the band director, helping make sure that everyone was following their patterns. This time around, Marquise, a friend and fellow drum major, climbed up on the podium, ready to lead the band through our set. That's when I heard it, a sentence that still makes me shudder to this day.

"Get that n—— off the podium!"

I looked behind me, peering into the home team's stands, a sea of white people there to watch a high school football game. There was too much other commotion to figure out who said it. My stomach sank. Did Marquise hear it? Did any of the other band members, most of whom were black? I glanced nervously at the band director to see if she'd heard it. The grimace on her face suggested she had. I didn't know what to do. She didn't either, it seemed. So we did nothing. The band began playing and the show, as they say, went on.

My band director and I spoke about the incident later, wondering what the hell had happened. As far as she could tell, no one in the band had heard it, and it seemed that nothing good would come from bringing it up. But from then on, we would no longer perform at away games. The school determined that it was too risky, deep in North Carolina, to bring a primarily African American band to rural areas where that kind of invective might be spewed at high school kids.

Then there was the annual Statesville Christmas Parade, when downtown Statesville transformed a mile-long stretch of Center Street into a winter wonderland, with parents bringing children in festive clothes to watch a procession of antique cars, floats, and performances from the 120-member Statesville High School Marching Band. Each year, one of the drum majors was given the special honor of dressing up as Santa Claus, a role that guaranteed applause from the kids standing along the side of the road. It was my turn to play Santa, and I had been looking forward to it.

But in the frantic few minutes before the parade, Marquise asked, "Hey, Rob, how about I play Santa this year?"

I was busy making sure everyone had their sheet music and uniforms squared away, so I had little time to contemplate Marquise's request.

"Sure, why not?" I shrugged. "I'll be an elf."

Marquise and I switched costumes. He took the red and white hat, and I took the green pointed cap. With the band in formation, we stepped off, providing a holiday-themed soundtrack to the day's festivities.

Halfway through the parade, I noticed that in addition to the laughter and delight from the kids, the adults were doing double takes. Some nudged one another, pointing at the band and shaking their heads. At first I was confused. Were we out of step? Was one of us doing something inappropriate?

I scanned the band to make sure we were all in line. We were. I looked at the other drum majors. They were keeping time, just as they should have been. Marquise was conducting and perfectly executing his role as Santa. He'd look over the crowd between songs with a big smile on his face, waving to the kids. Nothing out of the ordinary.

Then I stopped and again looked at Marquise. My stomach dropped. Suddenly, I understood what was causing the commotion. The white people of Statesville weren't ready for a black Santa Claus. (This was a few years before former Fox News host Megyn Kelly went on national television and declared, erroneously, that both Jesus and Santa were white.) I was heartbroken for Marquise, that this moment of holiday fun would be marred by the prejudices of our community.

I'm not sure if he saw the same things as me, but he seemed a bit flustered after the parade. Our band director, who always went out of her way to make sure all students, black and white, felt comfortable and safe during practices and events, took us aside and suggested that the last-minute switch maybe hadn't been the best idea, given the context of the parade. She wasn't mad about a black Santa, but she was upset that she hadn't been able to shield us from the not-so-veiled bigotry on display that day. When I talked with Marquise recently to check my facts on this story, he remarked how the sneers and jeers that day still remind him of how haunting racism in our little town can be. Before I received my driver's license, he would often drive me to my house in the country club. One time he was pulled over in the community by an officer simply because he "looked out of place."

That moment at the parade should have been as good as it gets in Statesville, a group of students bonding over service to the community, providing some free holiday cheer to kick off the season. Instead, it became the scandal of the Christmas season.

The message was reiterated a year later, when the parade organizers sent our band director a letter. Because of the "controversy" the previous year, which they declined to name, no Santa costumes would be allowed in that year's parade. There would be one Santa, on a float, played by an actor of the committee's choosing. Though they didn't say it, the intent was clear: In Statesville, Santa Claus is white.

EVEN THOUGH Statesville remains a place where a black Santa can cause consternation, there are also moments of grace when the community comes together and the issue of racism takes something of a break, an armistice in the protracted battle to eliminate this sin from our society.

One of my closest friends, Abbey, wasn't in the band, but she would faithfully attend each halftime show, cheering on her friends who marched and helping us out by carrying props and music. We spent lots of time hanging out after football games at Chili's or the Waffle House. Abbey was always good for a laugh, providing an escape from the heaviness that often accompanies high school.

On Halloween morning, 2009, I received a phone call telling me that Abbey had died in a car accident.

"We're all heartbroken," Scarlett Perry said, she was a close friend of Ellen Tsumas, Abbey's mother, her voice was wavering on the other end of the line. "But we have to plan the funeral. I know you and Abbey were close. Would you be willing to preach at the service?"

I was only seventeen, one of my closest friends had just died, and I was being asked to find the strength to help console a grieving community. Without giving it much thought—which no doubt would have made me hedge—I said yes.

"Thanks, Rob. It would've meant a lot to Abbey. . . . I know how much you meant to her."

All week, I prayed to find the right words that could bring hope to the darkness.

On the day of the funeral, more than one thousand people packed the church to celebrate Abbey's life and grieve her death. It was probably the most racially diverse group of people the white First Baptist Church had seen since its inception. The response showed the best of Statesville. People held one another and cried. I preached from Psalm 126, pushing my own emotion down so that I could keep it together up in the pulpit:

> *When the Lord restored the fortunes of Zion, we were like those who dream.*
> *Then our mouth was filled with laughter, and our tongue with shouts of joy;*
> *then it was said among the nations, "The Lord has done great things for them."*
> *The Lord has done great things for us, and we rejoiced.*
> *Restore our fortunes, O Lord, like the watercourses in the Negeb.*
> *May those who sow in tears reap with shouts of joy.*
> *Those who go out weeping, bearing the seed for sowing, shall come home with shouts of joy, carrying their sheaves.*

After reading the Psalm, I spoke of Abbey's laughter, of her joy, of how much it meant that a popular girl like her went out of her way to befriend a drum major kid like me. When she and I met, I was already engrossed in a world of theological reflection, which isn't exactly considered cool at seventeen. But Abbey would ask deep questions of faith that always challenged me.

I told the congregation how Abbey had always day-dreamed about her wedding day—and while that dream would never come true for her, in some small way, she was being wed to eternity that day. Then, together as a community, we commended her to God.

When the service wrapped up, the predominantly black drum line made its way to the front steps of the stone church. Standing on each side of the church doors under the crisp November sun, my bandmates played their cadences brilliantly and loudly as mourners made their way out of the church, many of whom belonged to the mostly white congregation. It was a chance for them to enjoy the drum line Abbey had loved so much in life. Perhaps the most heartbreaking moment came at the end, when Abbey's grief-stricken family made their way out of the church and down the stone stairs.

I'm not sure anyone thought about how the black drummers had given their time and energy to console those grieving inside an almost all-white church. But looking back, I see that even in death, Abbey was able to provide Statesville a grace-filled moment of racial reconciliation. It was not lost on me that some fifty years before this moment, the Reverend J. C. Harris, pastor of the predominately black First Baptist Church Incorporated, had led a "pray-in" on the lawn of that very same white

First Baptist Church, protesting the sinful segregation of its pews.

THERE HAVE BEEN other moments of grace, as well, even if they came only after painful reflection. Just before graduation, I met with our school principal one last time. During my four years at Statesville High School, Larry Rogers had been someone whose insight and wisdom I came to admire. A bald man with a thick mustache and always sporting a crisp suit and a pair of aviator sunglasses, Mr. Rogers always encouraged me to be myself.

"You've said you feel awkward about living in the country club and having things in life that other kids don't," I remember him observing. "Well, don't let that stop you. Form friendships with others who might not have as much as you do. You'll be surprised at the wealth of wisdom they can offer you. Don't ever forget what you said at Abbey's funeral and the impact it had on our community—you have a bright future. Don't let things like privilege prevent you from seeing your own soul."

Mr. Rogers resisted accepting the status quo in town—and he challenged us to do the same. You don't like that black students and white students appear not to interact much during the school day? Mr. Rogers would tell you to join a club where there was a lot of interaction. For me, that was the marching band.

Before our final meeting, I bought Mr. Rogers an expensive cigar from the shop where I worked as a cashier. This cigar shop was the largest humidor in North Carolina, a hot spot for locals and truck drivers making their way up and down I-77. During my year or so of working there, it quickly became apparent to me that the cigar shop was a safe space of sorts for white people. The men routinely made hateful jokes about the Obama family, took digs at black people, and shared nasty comments about how white people were bearing the brunt of our nation's hardships. My job was to ring up customers—not to make a fuss. But what I heard from the men sitting in the small lounge near the register made me furious, and their disregard for the people of color who walked into the store only proved that the deep chasm of race still divided us, even in a place as innocuous as a cigar store.

One gentleman of color—a regular customer— routinely tried to sit among the patrons in the big red lounge chairs. Immediately the tone and attitude of the conversation would change from boisterous laughter to hushed whispers between friends. It was obvious that this man was not welcome, and I felt awful for him. But I was a young white man, safely ensconced behind the counter. Unsure of what to do, I did nothing. These were fully grown men, and I was not brave enough to confront them. I did nothing. I knew I was wrong, that I was choosing to be complicit in the racism that soaks so much of our life down here. It's a feeling I let wash over me, unpleasant at the time but important to remember years later when I am tempted to take the easier path and do nothing.

When I gave Mr. Rogers the cigar at our final meeting, he thanked me and offered a bit of parting wisdom. He told me that I'd face many challenges in life, but that I should never shrink away from them. Instead, I should remember the lessons I had learned at Statesville High, both the graced moments and the painful ones, and be the best person I could be. He invoked the image of a shining city on the hill, saying that we should strive to show others the best of what we have to offer, never settling for the status quo or giving in to our worst impulses.

Life is filled with challenges for everybody, and I can understand how it would be easy to focus on the anger and bitterness, to head to a local cigar shop and whine about the hardships facing me and mine. Giving into anger is often the path of least resistance. But instead, I've tried to heed Mr. Roger's call to action and remember the moments when the black and white students at Statesville High were one, whether performing a halftime show, bringing Christmas cheer to small kids, or burying a dear friend. That is the Statesville, and the South, that I choose to remember.

One day, a week before Abbey died, she and I skipped class to go drink bottles of Cokes at the local restaurant. In that moment, I felt that our lives would be endless. Little did I know she would lose her life on earth a week later. But I think the optimism I felt that day teaches a valuable lesson, one that I think translates well here. I don't know if Statesville will ever fully evolve, or if the South will become a place where the best of this region can be enjoyed by all, fully reaching its potential. But I know deep down that the possibilities are endless. I know the chances and opportunities are as infinite as that day when I drank bottled Cokes with my friend for the last time. The task of the Southerner, the task of white people, the task of humankind is to realize that change and work for it.

Years later, I was sitting with my wife and our friend Nina at a local watering hole, and Nina said something that immediately felt deeply true: "You either learn from the problems of Statesville and leave, or you don't learn from them and you stay." We must escape the insurmountable odds of a place like Statesville and decide to confront the racist undertones of small-town rural America. Though Nina was right about people leaving this place, my wife and I have bucked the status quo and have made our home in a place with a lackluster economy, a place where brokenness is common, and the light seems dim. This can be difficult for Southerners, no matter their race.

With all this in mind, I realize the most essential truth of our existence: I lost Janie before I could say goodbye, and I lost Abbey far too soon. Don't let death bring you to reconciliation with God or one another. The choice and chance for change is now. We can and must be better. People's lives depend on it.

8

American history is longer, larger, more various,
more beautiful, and more terrible than anything
anyone has ever said about it.

—JAMES BALDWIN

MY YEARS AT Duke Divinity School, when I
was training to be a pastor, required some time to
focus on my mental health. For my entire life, I have struggled with anxiety and bipolar II disorder, both of which
seemed to strike just as I was readying myself for a life of
ministry and service. As a result, I wasn't able to dive into
the theological battles and fight for social justice in ways
that I would have liked. But there is one experience from
college and seminary that has stuck with me, one that
showed me that undertaking this kind of work is reward-
ing, but is often complete with its own set of challenges.

Part of seminarian formation includes being placed
at a church to gain valuable on-the-job experience. In
North Carolina we call it field education, and it's easy to
place students. There are plenty of faith communities for

aspiring ministers down here, and most of the senior pastors are grateful for the help. I had my eyes on the Cadillac of Methodist churches, one right in the middle of Raleigh, in the shadow of the old state capitol.

This particular church has something of a fascinating history. According to a booklet published in 1961 to celebrate its history, the church traces its roots to 1811, and was the first Methodist church in the state capital. The following year, it had seventy-six members, more than half of whom were black—this at a time when slavery was still alive and well in North Carolina. In the 1850s, white worshippers who attended the church decided African American slaves needed their own place of worship, and that's how the church down the road, St. Paul's, came to be. Then in the 1860s, this church's pastor took leave to serve in the Confederate army, with the support of his flock.

By the time I made my way here, in the summer of 2016, the church was four thousand members strong—and overwhelmingly white. The senior pastor at the time invited me to shadow him and learn the nitty-gritty of being a minister. He was getting ready to retire that summer, and I was eager to learn from his lifetime of experience. He's a hero in these parts, and he taught me the basics of running a church, how to conduct myself in sometimes-tense church meetings, and how to provide pastoral care to people facing difficult challenges.

When I was given the opportunity to preach, I decided to swing for the fences.

That summer, notorious cases of police brutality against African American men had come to light, including some cases that resulted in death. Outrage was palpable. Many black men said they feared for their lives during interactions with police, episodes that white people would see only as one of life's mere aggravations. Some families of black men said they worried that being pulled over might result not in a ticket, but in a shootout. I mustered up my courage and decided to not only preach about this to the church community, but to encourage my fellow ministers to do the same. To help get that message across, I wrote an essay for *The Washington Post.*

"I can't do much about what that Robert Lee did in the 19th century. But this Robert Lee can do something different today," I wrote. "As a Christian pastor, on Sunday, this descendant of the Lees of Virginia will step into a pulpit in Raleigh, N.C., and say the names 'Alton Sterling' and 'Philando Castile.' Because enough is enough."

Alton Sterling was killed by police officers in Baton Rogue, Louisiana, in the early morning hours of July 5, 2016. The following day, Philando Castile was killed by police in Minnesota during a traffic stop. Emotions were raging, protests were held in cities, and even President Obama weighed in.

"When places of worship give voice to what has happened," I wrote, "we can begin the long road to healing, to change and to the fruition of God's unfolding future."

In the hours after my essay was published, my phone

buzzed. It was a text message from one of the associate pastors.

"Be careful," he wrote. "A lot of people are talking about your article and I don't want to see you hurt."

Having spent more time in public ministry than me at that point, the associate pastor was well aware of the land mines present when discussing race from the pulpit. He was worried I'd say something wrong and find myself in trouble.

"Thanks," I said, appreciative of the warning but not planning to back down.

The next morning, I made my way to the church, planning to deliver the sermon from my heart. There were no notes. Instead I would rely on the passion burning inside me.

As I vested for the service, a senior member of the staff called me over.

"Rob," I remember him saying, "I wish you would have talked to me before publishing that essay."

"Oh?" I replied, caught a bit off guard.

He explained that because I was associated with the church—I had included my summer placement in my author bio at the *Post*—I needed to make sure I was representing the church's views in public.

"And the church isn't against racism?" I thought to myself.

Maybe it isn't, I considered. After all, their church

was completing a major building project even as the black church down the road that had once been associated with it was in severe need of capital improvements. Then again, this reluctance to engage could also be a survival tactic by older clergy not wanting to make a fuss or put their pensions in jeopardy. But I decided not to get into it, with the choir already warming up and me needing to preserve my mental energy for the sermon.

"I'm sorry," I conceded, more to move past this uncomfortable moment than anything else.

I delivered my remarks, saying the names like I promised and exhorting the congregation to fight for racial reconciliation. A few people thanked me afterward, but word eventually got back to me that more than a few people were upset.

My anxiety set in. Maybe I was wrong to push too much? Maybe I wasn't the right person to deliver this message? Was I being too hard on this community, who, after all, were graciously hosting me for the summer? I suffered a panic attack and wondered if my desired vocation wasn't the right fit after all.

As the weeks unfolded, my responsibilities at the church seemed to decrease. I was told this was because of changes in staffing, related to the senior pastor's departure, but I can't help but wonder if the essay and my sermon made those in power, the white people who control so much of the Christian experience in this country, uneasy. It can be hard for people to risk everything they have built for something that, at first glance, doesn't benefit them directly.

I'm not sure I recognized it at the time, but my experience at this church provided a valuable lesson about the perils of speaking up when saying nothing would be far easier. Working in this field, I've seen firsthand the sacrifices people of color make when speaking for justice. The insults hurled at them during protests, the threats they receive from angry white folk, and the hurt they experience when that nagging voice says, "You are not good enough." White Christians, who have such a place of privilege in our society, must be willing to make a fraction of that sacrifice to speak out against injustice, even if it isn't always easy. It was a lesson that would soon come in handy as I took my first post as a solo pastor for a tiny United Church of Christ congregation near Winston-Salem.

Winston is a sprawling city by Southern standards, but the church was located in a town of about 1,400 people in the middle of the Tar Heel State's onetime furniture-making mecca.

By the time I arrived in 2017, those thriving industrial days were long gone. Instead of robust factories churning out couches and dining sets, the town was struggling, part of the large swath of America that feels left behind by globalization and the concentration of wealth in urban areas.

When I interviewed for the position, I was still a student at Duke, about 140 miles east. I had already been active in progressive circles, and the lessons I learned about racism in Statesville were an ingrained part of me, so I wasn't sure what I would encounter in rural Davidson County. During the interview process, one person remarked that he was looking forward to then-president-elect Donald Trump following through on his promise to return jobs to places like Winston-Salem. Later, during a Sunday school session, my wife overheard a white man telling churchgoers that he had seen firsthand a white police officer helping a stranded black motorist change her tire.

"This," he said, "is further proof that racism is a thing of the past."

Episodes like this made me uneasy about the job, but most of the people I encountered seemed bighearted and eager to revitalize their struggling church.

The first few weeks were pretty typical for a new pastor. I spent time getting to know the worshippers, trying to understand the local culture and learn what the congregation envisioned for its future. The churchgoers were honest about their struggles of wanting to reach out to the community. They provided care to shut-ins in town, but for some reason they could never transform into a model church for the outside world. They had hired me for precisely this reason, to help their small community of faith reach outside the known and bring the Gospel to the wider community. In my mind, that mission included helping to bridge the racial divisions that still exist in North Carolina. This was so important to me and to some members of the congregation that I devoted a Sunday sermon, pretty early in my tenure, to the topic.

"Y'all *means all*," I proclaimed from the pulpit.

The message was simple enough: If we're going to be a welcoming church, we've got to open the doors to everyone. No exceptions.

Some folks nodded in approval, but others looked blankly ahead. I had known the message wouldn't resonate with everybody in the congregation. Before the service began, an older gentleman and regular churchgoer saw the name of my sermon printed out in the worship aid: "Y'all Means All."

He muttered to himself, perhaps a bit too loudly, "He's not really gonna do this, is he?"

I did—and I could tell the message didn't land. I was so frustrated. I knew there were good members of that church who wanted it to grow, who prayed that our faith community could live out the Gospel values in real and concrete ways. That's why they'd brought me in, to help them get outside of their comfort zone. But when push came to shove, when I preached a sermon about welcoming everyone, just as Jesus had asked of his followers, it didn't seem to click. It wasn't that people told me off or stormed out. It's what they didn't say. It was back to business as usual. I didn't know it at the time, but this experience would serve as a trial run for the work that was to come.

A FEW MONTHS into my tenure at the church, white America's collective rage boiled over during a hate-fueled rally of white supremacists in Virginia.

At issue was a statue of General Lee that stands in a park named for him, just down the road from the University of Virginia. The protests that August were the culmination of events that began a year before, when a sixteen-year-old black woman wrote a petition aimed at city officials to ask them to remove the statue and change the name of the park.

"As a teenager in Charlottesville that identifies as black, I am offended every time I pass it," wrote Zyahna Bryant. "I am reminded over and over again of the pain of my ancestors and all the fighting that they had to go through for us to be where we are now."

Ms. Bryant's letter was championed by some local officials who wanted to take action on the matter, which sparked a months-long debate about the future of the memorial. Like many statues honoring Lee and other Civil War figures, the one in Charlottesville was built long after the Civil War ended. In this case, it was donated to the city in the 1920s, with the resurgence or second emergence of the KKK, it was a time when black Americans still had their rights blatantly and routinely restricted by unjust laws and institutions. But not everyone in town bought the argument that statues of Lee and his fellow Southerners were racist. Charlottesville real estate attorney Lewis

Martin III, for example, told *The New Yorker* that the people who supported the statues when they were built were concerned with honoring the dead, not slavery.

"They were thinking about the veterans of the Civil War whom they knew personally, and the generals whom they considered heroes," he said.

The town was torn, and as the case received publicity through news reports and social media, a group of white supremacists took notice. They then planned to gather in Charlottesville to protest attempts to remove that particular statue and others like it. The "Unite the Right" rally was aimed at young white men who see the growing acceptance of people of different races, religions, and ethnicities as a threat, rather than an opportunity. In reality, the rally was about more than statues. It was about reminding people of color that they ought to live in fear.

The night before the rally was to take place, hundreds of people of different faiths gathered inside Saint Paul's Memorial Church to talk about ways they could protest the rally or serve as peaceful counter witness to the hate that would be on display the next morning. They had been preparing for months, aware of the possible violence. But some of them reported being shocked that night when hundreds of angry young men marched past the church carrying lit TIKI torches, headed to a statue of President Thomas Jefferson nearby. The group chanted, "You will not replace us!" along with "Jews will not replace us!" and clashed with a small group of counterprotesters who had gathered at the monument. When things started to escalate, with a TIKI-torch canister being thrown into the crowds, police stepped in and broke up the demonstration. There was a relatively peaceful end to the events that night. But it wouldn't last.

The next morning, hundreds of white supremacists gathered in Lee Park to pay homage to one of their heroes—my distant uncle, the man whose mythology I have grappled with since my conversation with Mrs. Bertha more than a decade ago. The counterprotesters, led by about twenty members of the clergy of varying faiths, along with other activists, including some from Black Lives Matter, took their spots nearby. Skirmishes broke out all morning, and social media feeds were filled with frightening scenes in which men with large guns tried to intimidate black protesters and praying clergy. Before the day was out, the governor of Virginia had declared a state of emergency.

The scene played out for hours, images of hate making their way through social media. Then, toward the end of the day, one of the white supremacists plowed his car into a group of counterprotesters. Several people were knocked down and injured. One young woman, Heather Heyer, was struck by the car, and her leg was caught underneath it. When the driver reversed, Heather was dragged for several feet. After the driver fled the scene, the extent of the carnage was made visible. Heather was bleeding badly from her leg. Medical workers and clergy rushed to aid her and the other victims, but Heather wouldn't survive her injuries. She, along with two police officers who were killed when their helicopter crashed outside of Charlottesville, succumbed to a day of hate.

Following the violence, Charlottesville's mayor, who had been ambivalent about the statues, changed his mind and said they should be removed. The city council decided that they should be covered with tarps until then, to remove the incendiary images from public view. But as the months wore on, some people wanted their statues back. About six months after the hate-fueled rally, a judge said the coverings were meant to be temporary and ordered them removed. The city complied. The Virginia chapter of the Sons of the Confederate Veterans cheered, calling the ruling a victory. The statues, at least as of this writing, remain up, a sad homage to a violent time in our nation's past—and now, its present.

When I saw those images of angry young white men marching with fire and spewing hate, a range of emotions flooded my mind. I was angry for the people of color in my life who, once again, were subjected to violent images flashing across screens. I thought of the moments of grace I had experienced in the South, and was saddened that the ugly side of our culture once again dominated the headlines. But most important, I had to fight the temptation to give into fear and do nothing. I knew I had to step up and contribute something to the wider conversation. Too many people of color have led the way for me, helped to educate me about justice, and gave of their time and energy when it would have been easier for them to do nothing.

I was sitting in my condo answering some emails when a message popped up from a producer at NPR. She explained that one of the anchors had read an interview I gave to the *Huffington Post* and wanted to talk.

"Hey, Steph," I said to my wife, "NPR wants to talk. Yikes."

Normally, accepting an opportunity to bring a message of peace and racial reconciliation to a wide audience would be a no-brainer. A preacher has to be prepared for any pulpit. But I had been taken aback and a little spooked by some of the reaction to the interview that had caused NPR to reach out. The *HuffPost* reporter had asked about my views on statues of Robert E. Lee, and I gave my standard answer, that they should come down and that it saddens me that my family name is being used to inspire hate. Then, several emails arrived.

"You need to be quiet," one said.

"You're treading on dangerous grounds," read another.

The messages were vaguely threatening, but in an oddly Southern way. The words almost sounded kind, as if the senders were worried about the trouble I'd face if I kept making noise about these issues. But peel back that veneer of politeness and the message was clear: If you're gonna keep it up, watch out.

Though I never considered going silent, I hedged a bit when it came time to accept an interview for a wider audience. Intimidation, even when brushed off for the silliness it is, has a way of lurking in the back of our minds and preying on our self-doubt. Stephanie, though, a journalist by training, said the NPR interview would be a good chance to spread a message of justice and reconciliation.

"I don't know, maybe I'm not the right person for this," I said, still unsure.

She'd have none of it. "You're doing it."

Stephanie, as usual, was right. This was a chance to highlight racial bigotry and challenge the way others in the South handled themselves.

So on a Thursday afternoon, I hopped in my Jeep and made the short drive to the studio where the interview would take place. After a quick tour, the sound engineer sat me down in front of the microphone, instructed me to put on a pair of headphones, and patched me into the national NPR desk. By the time the host came on the line, my nerves had calmed, and I actually enjoyed the conservation.

The interviewer started by asking the question on everyone's mind that summer: Should statues honoring heroes of the Confederacy, including those honoring General Lee, come down? Having anticipated the question, I answered straightforwardly.

"I do think they need to come down," I said. "I think

it's time that we have a conversation about how to remember our past without commemorating our past."

She then asked about my work as a pastor, and I explained to her that idolatry in any form is prohibited by the Gospels.

"We have made an idol of Robert Edward Lee. We have made him an idol of white supremacy. We have made him an idol of nationalism and of bigotry and of hate and of racism. And that's unacceptable."

Despite the threats people had aimed at me online, I said, I felt I needed to take a stand, "so that, going forward, they can say, there was a Lee who stood up for what's right instead of standing up for the wrong side of history."

When we finished, I thanked the engineers and headed home. Back to the day-to-day work of teaching and preaching, I thought.

Come Sunday morning, Stephanie and I were so lost in our normal routine—preparing breakfast, reading the news, and getting ready for church—that I had forgotten the interview was scheduled to air. It was only when Stephanie frantically told me to turn on the radio that a bit of anxiety returned. The interview started a minute or two later. Afterward, I looked at Stephanie to see what she'd made of it. She smiled at me and congratulated me on a job well done. I felt I had contributed to the dialogue, explained why I believed what I did, and hopefully challenged some folks in the South to consider another point of view. Still, I had a nagging suspicion that this was about to become bigger than a single radio interview.

That's when I heard from Mother Aleen. She had heard the interview, and she wanted to tell me I had done well. And just like she had warned before, way back at the MLK breakfast, she told me to be careful, that things were about to get hard for me. Not exactly comforting words, but she turned out to be right.

A few days after the interview aired, more threats started rolling in. Only this time, they seemed more menacing.

"You're treading on the graves of Confederate soldiers," read one email. "Be careful, or one day you might end up like that."

Criticism about "treading on graves" is common in the South. White Southern culture reveres our history. That is, the sanitized version of our history. For certain folks down here, Confederate soldiers aren't rebels or traitors— they are American heroes. It takes some elaborate mental gymnastics to arrive at this interpretation of history, but once you're there, it's not ground you want to give up. So when anyone dares to criticize the South, or the Confederacy, or the symbols of that period in history that still dot this landscape—or even tries to offer a more complete picture of our history—the "treading on graves" language comes out. But threatening, however vaguely, to put me in one of those graves was something new. And it wasn't pleasant.

The email messages were scary enough, but things were taken to a new level when a letter arrived in my parents' mailbox, addressed to my father.

"You better educate your boy," it read. "He needs to learn his history." My father scanned it over quickly and looked to see who sent it, but of course it wasn't signed. Again, in typical Southern fashion, the letter didn't come right out and threaten my parents or me. Southerners are too polite for that. Instead, the message was vague enough to seem harmless but clear enough in its intent to get the meaning across: *Watch it.*

My parents eventually called the local police chief to let him know what was going on. We weren't scared, but we were aware enough of how speaking out for racial justice in the South can sometimes lead to acts of violence. Because of the letter my dad received, I worried for my family and was saddened that they were being dragged into a fight they didn't pick. But they assured me that they supported my work, and urged me to ignore the noise and focus on the mission at hand.

So I did my best. On Monday afternoon, I was back in the classroom at a state university in the mountains of North Carolina, ready to begin a public speaking course and a religion course I'd been hired to teach after one of the professors fell ill.

Just as class was about to start, I glanced down at my iPhone. That's when I saw it: an email from an executive at MTV, asking if I'd be up for a last-minute trip to

Los Angeles to appear on the Video Music Awards. With my students seated in front of me, I spent the next ninety minutes teaching while simultaneously wondering if I was being punked—or if my ministry was about to link arms with an incredibly unlikely partner.

WHEN I TALKED with Noopur Agarwal, MTV's vice president for social impact, she explained that I would fly to Los Angeles the next morning and appear on the show alongside Susan Bro, the mother of Heather Heyer, the social justice activist killed in Charlottesville. The brass at MTV thought that Susan and I appearing together would send a powerful message to the millions of young people watching the awards show.

When I hung up with Noopur, the voices of doubt started coming back.

"Don't do it, Rob. Who do you think you are? You aren't up for the task. Besides, it's more trouble than it's worth."

I was still relatively new to this public fight for social justice conversation. Grappling with my own family's legacy was an ongoing process, and I wasn't sure I was ready for such a big platform. But when I turned to my dad for advice, I had hardly begun to explain the invitation when he interjected.

"When do you leave?" he asked.

"Uh, I'm going?" I asked, a bit confused.

"Of course you are!" he shot back.

"Okay, then," I thought to myself, "I guess I'll call Stephanie." When I got ahold of her, she didn't believe that the invitation was real. I started expressing my doubts about the whole thing, but once again, she would have none of it.

"Rob, you're going. And I need to get something to wear."

It was settled, then. I guess I had my marching orders.

I called Noopur back and told her we were in. She said a team of writers would be in touch to help me craft a minute-long message, but I offered to take a crack at it myself. She explained that MTV would take care of the logistics and that she'd be there to greet us in Los Angeles the next day. Then, Stephanie and I set off for the two-hour drive to Charlotte so she could find a new dress. I thought about buying a new shirt or tie, but Stephanie, once again, was more clearheaded.

"You've just been handed one of the biggest pulpits in the world," she told me. "You're wearing a black shirt and a collar."

The whole trip to L.A. was surreal. I'm a small-town boy who grew up in the Piedmont of North Carolina. I never once thought I'd appear on a show that airs in half a billion households in 170 countries—much less be flown first-class to Los Angeles to get there. Once we boarded, I typed out an email to Noopur with the words I hoped to deliver on Sunday night. I hit send just as the flight attendants finished their safety demonstration, and we were off.

The next day, we had a rehearsal at the Forum, the indoor arena located right outside Los Angeles where the awards show would take place. I met Susan Bro and told her how sorry I was for the loss of her daughter, which had happened only two weeks earlier. She nodded, but she told me I should not apologize. Instead, she thanked me for speaking out for justice. This was one of the most humbling moments of my life, that this mother who had suffered such an unjust loss was thanking me simply for saying what was right. I told her how much I admired her courage, and we pledged that we would stay in touch. Maybe there was something more we could do together to continue the work.

That night, at dinner, Stephanie asked how I was feeling.

"Good!" I told her. Much to my relief, that was the honest-to-God truth.

The scriptwriters accepted my words verbatim, which heartened me. It meant the message I delivered would be my own, one that I had been working and reworking my entire life. I knew my cues and felt ready to go. Most important, I was being given a chance to preach a message of peace and reconciliation to millions. 5.62 million to be exact when the final numbers came in.

But when morning came, I was a nervous wreck. I paced the hotel room, trying to memorize my speech even though I had rehearsed with the teleprompter the day before. I was scared, not that I'd mess up my lines, but for others. I worried about the backlash my family in Statesville might experience. I was afraid Stephanie might be attacked for being married to me. And most of all, I was worried that I wasn't the right messenger, that I didn't have what it takes to speak about such weighty issues.

But my mind went to the book of Esther, a text that a close friend had preached at my ordination. In that portion of text, Mordecai challenges his cousin not to stay silent when an evil man, Haman, plots to destroy the Jewish race. The case is being tried in the court of Esther's husband, the Persian king Artaxerxes, but Esther is afraid of what will happen if she intervenes.

"If you remain silent, help will arise from another quarter," Mordecai tells Esther. "But who knows? Perhaps you have come to this position for such a time as this." This was the passage Stephanie and I read right before we stepped out of the hotel room and into the elevator. I had a weird feeling, remembering back to the day when the Reverend Nathan Kirkpatrick, a mentor and close friend, Stephanie, and a host of clergy laid hands on me and asked God to ordain me to ministry. Nathan looked me in the eyes with a deep love and said that Stephanie and I would be accountable to the world in a new way. Like Mother Aleen's prediction, I thought they were flattering words, but that's what you're supposed to say. Maybe people like Nathan and Mother Aleen had seen something at work in me that I hadn't. But the time for that wasn't now. The elevator doors open and the cameras started to flash.

As we pulled up and saw the throngs of media gathered to cover the show, fear and anxiety washed back over me. The look on my face changed. Stephanie knew what was going on. She took my hand.

"You've got this, my love," she said.

Inside, dozens of MTV staff gave us credentials and got us settled in the green room. The whole place was swarming with celebrities. When a young woman approached me and thanked me for my work, I responded graciously and asked what she does for a living. She told me she worked in the music business. I wished her well and we went our separate ways. That's when I noticed my phone buzzing. A text from Stephanie across the way.

"You were just chatting with Kesha!" she had written.

I looked over at her and shrugged. I had no idea.

Before long, it was time for Susan and I to go on. I walked to the stage, a futuristic, geometric backdrop lit up in dark blue lights behind. The packed arena fell silent, and though it was just a few seconds, it felt like an eternity. My nerves were creeping up again, so I reminded myself: "You've been given this chance, you have a voice, now is the time to use it." A red light turned on, a signal from a producer, and we were live.

"My name is Robert Lee IV. I'm a descendant of Robert E. Lee, the Civil War general whose statue was at the center of violence in Charlottesville," I said.

The crowd was silent, an eerie feeling at an awards show for music videos. But I continued on.

"We have made my ancestor an idol of white supremacy, racism, and hate. As a pastor, it is my moral duty to speak out against racism, America's original sin. Today, I call on all of us with privilege and power to answer God's call to confront racism and white supremacy head-on. We can find inspiration in the Black Lives Matter movement, the women who marched in the Women's March in January, and, especially, Heather Heyer, who died fighting for her beliefs in Charlottesville."

Then Susan took the stage to a much-deserved standing ovation. I clapped, too, in awe of her strength to be here, her daughter's death still raw.

"Only fifteen days ago, my daughter Heather was killed as she protested racism," Susan said. "I miss her, but I know she is here tonight."

My heart was racing.

Susan announced that she would honor her daughter's fight for justice by establishing a foundation "to help more people join Heather's fight against hatred," adding that her daughter "never marched alone. She was always joined by people from every race and every background in this country."

We exited together, our part done for the evening. I felt at peace.

The after-party was held outside under a big tent. Stephanie and I spotted some celebrities, took our picture with Noopur, and grabbed some food, but ultimately decided we had to get out of there. The scene was chaotic, a bit too much for an introverted, overtired pastor from North Carolina.

Reflecting on the appearance afterward, I realized that the most compelling part of the evening was realizing that I was now connected to a community much larger than I could have imagined. I knew deep down that the racial injustices I witnessed growing up in Statesville were not right, but seeing this giant, international audience rally around a message of inclusion was a whole new experience. Meeting people like Susan Bro, who took her daughter's unjust death and somehow turned it into something positive—an opportunity to preach peace—gave me a glimmer of hope. And the reaction to her speech on social media, so much of it positive and encouraging, showed me how hungry people are for moral leadership. The hate on display in Charlottesville was powerful, with the potential to consume us. But Susan's simple plea for peace and justice was a strong antidote to the nihilism of white supremacy. It's a call to all of us to do better, to look at how each of us perpetuate injustice in our own lives. A simple message, but one that we haven't spent enough time incorporating into our lives. Mrs. Bertha had always told me that my pulpit wouldn't be in one locale, it would be spread across a range of places and circumstances. She, like Mother Aleen and Nathan, had a prophetic edge that I had never imagined would *really* take effect.

My phone buzzed and beeped in what felt like a non-stop onslaught of notifications following the VMAs. Family members and friends congratulated me on the appearance and offered me encouragement during what they assumed might be a difficult yet inspiring time. There were some hateful messages, too, but I tried to focus on the positive remarks, remembering that this wasn't about me—it was about the message of justice and equality laid down by others in my life. But as Stephanie and I took our seats for the long flight back across the country, a message appeared from one of the leaders in the congregation where I served. The email was short and to the point: "When you return, we need to talk."

I wasn't sure what this meant, but now I had more than five hours to imagine worst-case scenarios. That is one of the worst feelings for someone with anxiety, stuck in a metal tube hurtling across the skies of this country without Wi-Fi to fix or evade trouble. I felt helpless, unsure what I had done wrong and fearful for the first time that the reaction back home might not be as positive as I had hoped. I ordered a drink and tried to relax, but as soon as the plane touched down, I opened my phone and began a reply.

"Yes, let's talk about this soon," I wrote. But I needed to think over some things first.

I was eager to get back to the work God had called me to. Little did I know that the life Stephanie and I had known was about to change forever.

9

God will either shield you from suffering or
give you the unwavering strength to bear it.

—SAINT FRANCIS DE SALES

O VER THE COURSE of the next week, I realized my appearance on the VMAs had put my
fledgling ministry at risk.

The first indication that something was off came from
a review left on the church's Facebook page, which I ad-
ministered. We were a small church in a small town, the
kind of place where anonymity is a luxury residents aren't
allowed. Before the VMAs, the Facebook page had just a
couple dozen likes and even fewer reviews. When an alert
popped up and said a new review had been posted, I was
curious. I clicked on it, hoping for something positive, but
bracing for something hurtful.

A local resident who often attended service but wasn't
a member of the church had left a scathing review taking
issue with my support of Black Lives Matter. She wrote,

The church is led by pastor Robert Lee, who is an extremist with a very dangerous ideology. He tells others to find inspiration in the Black Lives Matter movement and those who participated in the Women's March. BLM, a movement whose followers openly call for and commit acts of violence against police officers. . . .

If you are looking for a church home who values the inclusiveness of *all* God's children, and church leaders who advocate peace, love, and compassion to help bring communities together, keep looking. Sadly this church is not it.

I was shocked by the blatant mischaracterization of the group, and I worried that others in the community felt the same. A deep sense of fear fell over me.

"I'm going to lose my job, aren't I?" I thought to myself.

Rather than give into the anxiety, I took a few deep breaths and reminded myself that this person was only one person. I thought of people like Mrs. Bertha and remembered the courage they had shown in their lives combating racism. A one-star review on Facebook paled in comparison to that. I decided to put the incident behind me and get on with my work.

But the floodgates had been opened. I was alerted to other social media posts. Some members of the church were taking issue with not only my appearance on MTV, but with the message of tolerance I preached—the "Y'all Means All" sermon, for example. Then, it happened. One of my worst fears came to fruition.

A member of the church emailed me to say that she thought I should resign, that I had become too toxic to minister effectively. Another church member suggested that I could attempt to bridge the divisions I had caused and recant what I had said by delivering a sermon or issuing a statement along the lines of "All lives matter." I was shocked. Before being hired, I had been open with the mostly white community that racial justice would be an important part of my ministry.

These people didn't have the authority to fire me, exactly. But they warned they would withhold donations and make the church's work difficult. I was saddened that they would threaten the community like this, all because of a message of inclusion I preached—a message that should not have been earth-shattering to hear coming from any preacher. My appearance on the VMAs may have been surprising, but the message I shared there was no different from the ones I had preached in our small church. Love trumps hate. The only difference was the size of the pulpit. I was shocked that members of the church would ask me to publicly renounce a belief like that.

Scared, upset, and more than a bit angry, I called Nathan. He had been a mentor for me ever since my early days of ministry, back when the thought of preaching on a Sunday filled me with dread brought on by my struggles with anxiety: *What would my message be? Did people care what a young pastor had to say?* Through it all, Nathan had assured me that God had placed me in this spot for a reason. During meetings with parishioners, whether to celebrate milestones like weddings or to provide solace during tough times, Nathan's reminder that I was doing what God had called me to do would stay at the front of my mind. But as I continued to grapple with the fallout from the VMA appearance, this counsel from my hero and friend was increasingly difficult to remember. So I called Nathan up at his Duke University office.

"What would you do if you were me?" I asked, eager for his advice.

Nathan thought it over for a minute. Then he suggested I resign.

"Resign?" I shot back. "I didn't think things were that bad!"

"You're too early in your career for a protracted battle with a community that might have its heart set on making you leave," he said. "It's just one job, and you'll need to be able to continue ministering elsewhere."

His words hurt. Had I failed? Wasn't speaking out for reconciliation part of my job?

"Just remember, Rob, this will all work out," he said. "Remember what I always tell you: You are beloved by God—and by me."

I talked it over with Stephanie that night, and together we decided Nathan was right. Rather than draw the small community into a public battle that could harm the congregation, I decided to offer my resignation to the church's board. The decision didn't come easily. Everything felt like it was moving so fast, and I cared for these people deeply. More selfishly, I was fresh out of grad school and newly married, so naturally I worried about money. And in the back of my mind, I wondered if it was cowardly to walk away from a community simply because I'd encountered a little resistance. All these considerations weighed heavily on me, but I felt that God was calling me to step down and allow the church to heal.

I informed church leaders of my plan, which was to leave in a few weeks, after tying up loose ends and saying goodbye to the congregation. After some back and forth, they accepted my resignation—but stipulated that it would be effective the following Sunday. I could use that service to bid farewell to the congregation, they told me.

I was stung by this response, but I agreed to the church's terms. A clean break might be the best option for Stephanie and me, and for the church community.

In the letter announcing my resignation, I wrote,

I regret that speaking out has caused concern and pain to my church. For this I offer my heartfelt apology. I understand that my views could be considered to be controversial. I never sought this sort of attention. But I do believe in God's role in calling out for positive social change for the good of all. We are all called by God to speak out against hate and evil in all its many forms. There are so many good things going on with this congregation, and I do not want my fight to detract from the mission. If the recent media attention causes concern with my church, I reluctantly offer my resignation.

That Sunday, I arrived at the small, redbrick church and looked up at the white steeple for one last time as its pastor. I had to remind myself that even amid all the confusion and the hurt, God was at work.

"It might not make sense now," I told myself, but eventually, I prayed, it would.

The announcement took many of the congregants by surprise. The nonverbal reactions were clear: Most had had no idea that there had been any trouble following my MTV appearance. But rather than go into details about the demands that had been made on me by their neighbors, I focused on the Gospel, exhorting the worshippers to continue working toward who God was calling them to be. When the service ended, I did what had become my routine for the past five months, standing in the back of the church to greet the congregation and listen to their stories. Some attendees expressed frustration and bewilderment with the circumstances of my departure, as others used their cellphones to try to reach some church leaders who had decided not to attend my farewell service.

I don't want to paint this picture as if the people of

that church were all maligned and filled with hate. There truly was a sense of movement and a willingness to try new things from some of the members. Right after I resigned, I received a lovely email from a couple who worshipped at the church, asking me to reconsider.

"You are a 'breath of fresh air' to our church," the email read.

The fresh air wasn't me, of course, but the message I preached, the Gospel. There were people in that community who understood the need to seek reconciliation. I may have pushed too hard at some points. But I knew we had to part ways. Engaging in the difficult work of racial reconciliation can have consequences. Maybe not always as dramatic as a job loss that goes public. But it may cause hurt or discomfort for people you care about. I took consolation in knowing, however, that there were some members back at the church who would continue the fight.

THE WEEKS FOLLOWING my departure were difficult and at times surreal. In an effort to distance themselves from me, the church asked me to announce my resignation publicly. A friend offered to help me with this by posting a statement on the website of the Auburn Seminary, a sort of think tank and school for progressive people of faith. In the statement, I reiterated my belief that as an indirect descendant of General Robert E. Lee, I felt it was my duty to speak out against white supremacy. I also acknowledged that the church's opinion had been split, highlighting both the positive and negative reactions I received following my public appearances:

> I want to stress that there were many in the congregation who supported my right to free speech, yet were uncomfortable with the attention the church was receiving. . . . I feel a deep love for this congregation, and gratitude that they were willing to hire me as my first church out of seminary. I believe with all my heart that God did good work in my life there.

> I do not want this episode to be a distraction from the sacred work of confronting white supremacy in all its forms. My calling and my vocation has led me to speak out against violence and oppression in any form, and I want to especially challenge white Christians in America to take seriously the deadly legacy of slavery in our country and commit ourselves to follow Jesus into a time of deep reflection, repentance and reconciliation.

The backlash to that statement, especially on social media, was at times harsh. But there were moments of grace in the days following my resignation. One of the more encouraging moments came on the very afternoon

I resigned, when Stephanie and I drove to Raleigh to visit her high school friend Claire. Claire's father is Roy Cooper, the Democratic governor of North Carolina. Claire invited Stephanie and me to join her family for a visit in the private residence of the governor's mansion, a rare honor for this North Carolina native who truly loves his home state. The governor and his daughter are a lot alike, both driven, concerned about the happenings of the day, and motivated to care for others.

That night, Mr. Cooper came across less like the governor of a large American state and more as a dad who was eager to learn about his daughter's friends. When he asked me how I was faring in my new role as a minister, unaware that I was newly unemployed and worried about our future, I filled him in on everything, including the experience at the VMAs and the hurtful reaction back home. He took a long moment to think, but then said he was proud of Stephanie and me for standing up for what we believe in, and assured us that we were on the right side of history. He told me that his travels to every corner of North Carolina had convinced him that there are more people who agree with the message of racial equality and justice than don't. It was a moment of grace that I sorely needed.

As Claire, Stephanie, and I walked around the grounds of the governor's mansion that day, I remember wanting to cry. But I also remember Claire, with her characteristic bigheartedness and empathy in full force, saying, simply, "Today sucks, but there is hope ahead."

The Cooper family had been through a lot in the 2016 election. It was a hard-fought race against a Republican incumbent . . . and no governor seeking reelection in North Carolina's history had ever been defeated. One of the main issues in the race was the so-called bathroom bill, a bigoted piece of legislation that required transgender people to use the bathrooms that corresponded with the sex on their birth certificates, rather than their gender identity. This meant that some people who identify as women would have to use men's rooms—and some who identify as men would have to use ladies' rooms. The bill made national headlines after the NCAA decided to stop holding championship events in North Carolina to protest the law. Some businesses, including PayPal, boycotted the state as well, which caused grievous harm to the state economy. But supporters of the law dug in, demonstrating that ignorance in the South is not limited to matters of race.

To his credit, Mr. Cooper opposed the law, known as House Bill 2. His critics said horrible things about him— that he supported the right of men to use the same bathrooms and locker rooms as girls and women, putting their safety at risk. The attacks were unfair and painful for the Cooper family, but they fought hard for what they believed in—and won. Mr. Cooper was elected governor by a razor-thin margin in what turned out to be the most expensive, not to mention one of the nastiest, gubernatorial campaigns in our state's history. Claire and her father had been through so much, but they pushed through and claimed victory on election night, a decision that provided hope for so many dismayed by the national election results.

If they could be resilient, then I could be as well.

That's the beauty of the South, resiliency is at our core. I would argue that progressive people in the South desperately want to see our region lifted up for its progress and its willingness to change. We all see the potential, but are sometimes left bogged down and spinning our wheels because the realities seem daunting, if not downright impossible to change.

IN THE MONTHS following my resignation, I've been privileged to visit churches throughout the South as a guest preacher. Other ministers have reached out to collaborate on efforts to combat racism in our nation and our church. More than the TV appearances and the glitzy parties chock-full of celebrities I don't recognize anyway, these visits to churches from Georgia to Virginia to New England and California are what sustain me.

It's easy for critics to dismiss these kinds of visits as all talk, no action. It's true there is a lot of talking! (Well, preaching, to be precise.) And informal conversations afterward. Shared meals. Listening. And dialogue. What shouldn't get lost is that these encounters are a relatively new phenomenon. That churches—white churches in the South and elsewhere—want to have these sometimes difficult conversations about race is a sign of progress. To be Christian means to believe that racial reconciliation is necessary to help redeem a fallen world. We all have a part to play.

One weekend, I invited a family member to attend a talk I gave at Spartanburg Methodist College in South Carolina. I preached about how we, the white church, had made white supremacy an idol. Later that night, this person texted my wife.

"Rob really made me think," he wrote.

That's the goal. We've got to get people thinking that the way things are now, no matter how long they've been like this, no matter how seemingly intractable our divisions seem, they don't need to be like this. These conversations, these small moments of grace, they remind me that we are interconnected in this mission to overcome our nation's original sin.

Another encounter took place in the overwhelmingly secular enclave of Cambridge, Massachusetts—perhaps the last place a Southern Christian preacher might turn for inspiration. It was here where I dined with the Reverend Professor Jonathan L. Walton, the Plummer Professor of Christian Morals at Harvard Divinity School and the Pusey Minister of the Memorial Church of Harvard University, an interfaith community situated at the center of one of the world's most elite power centers.

Jonathan invited me to guest preach one Sunday at the chapel. It was February 2018, five months after I left my church in North Carolina. I had already begun the preaching circuit that took me to pulpits around the United States, and had regained some of my footing, but to a boy from Statesville, the idea of preaching inside the rarefied halls of Harvard felt daunting. Jonathan invited Stephanie and me to have dinner the night before to welcome us to Cambridge.

Young and brilliant, Jonathan began teaching at Harvard in his thirties and was asked to take the helm of the Memorial Church just a few years later, in 2013. He grew up in Atlanta, where he learned about the invaluable role people of faith contributed to the civil rights movement.

But his knowledge of justice work came from more than theory. Earlier that year, he had required police protection after giving a powerful sermon in which he dubbed the National Rifle Association a "domestic terrorist organization."

"This nation is sick," Jonathan had preached, calling on Congress to do something to end the scourge of violence plaguing our communities. "Our cultural anxiety, toxic masculinity, and racial, religious, and ethnic bigotries are eating away at the soul of this nation."

As a reward for speaking his mind, Jonathan received more than one threat against his life.

Though just a little more than a decade or so older than me, Jonathan exudes a wisdom that comes from years of work in the social justice movement. He's a scholar, an activist, a strong yet gentle presence, and one of the hardest-working preachers I know. I couldn't wait to ask him all about the NRA ordeal—but when we met up with him in a restaurant on Harvard Square, he wanted to know how *we* were doing. Turns out being a minister at one of the most storied pulpits in America hadn't caused Jonathan to lose even one bit of his pastoral touch.

"Well, it's been a lot," Stephanie told him, recounting the loss of my job and the backlash we'd endured in the months since. "But it's our new normal."

Jonathan paused for a moment, then said, "It can never become the new normal."

We both looked at him, wanting more. And he delivered.

"Never let this be normal, because it isn't normal," he said. "You are not normal folk and God is not a normal god. We can't let this penetrate your house. Remember who your friends are and who you can rely on."

He didn't mean that Stephanie and I were more special than other people. Rather, he wanted to remind us that God desires more for us than the status quo. If we accept things as they are, if we resign ourselves to the omnipotence of hate and injustice, believing that nothing will change for the better, we've turned our backs on God's plan. If icons like the Reverend Dr. Martin Luther King, Jr., Rosa Parks, Malcolm X, Bayard Rustin, Ida B. Wells—the list goes on—had accepted the status quo, how much poorer would we be as a people?

On a much more personal scale, what if Mrs. Bertha

had just shrugged and said, "White Southern boys will be white Southern boys" when I told her I had a Confederate flag hanging in my bedroom, rather than telling me to take it down? It's impossible to know what would have happened, but had it not been for Mrs. Bertha's words that day, perhaps I wouldn't have examined my own life's path, or how my seemingly private actions influenced the lives of people I cared about.

Jonathan wasn't done—and we didn't want him to be.

"Think of your end game. What is it you want to accomplish?" he asked. "Focus on that. Don't let other things lure you away."

The next day, my family, both immediate and extended, joined me as I gave a lecture and preached a sermon at Harvard. As I made my way toward the imposing pulpit, Jonathan pulled me aside.

"Martin Luther King and Billy Graham have preached from that pulpit," he said with a grin. "But no pressure."

My stomach churned a little bit. But I climbed the stairs and took a deep breath. I paused for a quick second and looked out at my family and my wife. My gaze turned to Jonathan and the students and members of the Cambridge community who had gathered to hear God's message that day. The responsibility hung heavily on me, but I preached like the opportunity wasn't normal, just as Jonathan said. My message that day wasn't particularly memorable, especially compared to those who had preached at the same pulpit decades before me. But standing there, at just twenty-five years old, and preaching about the Trans-figuration was electric.

After the service, Stephanie and I went to lunch with our families. We talked about the service and the astounding music. But more important, for the first time, I realized I had made a difference in the lives of the people who mattered to me most: my family.

"Rob, what you said about statues got me thinking," my dad said. "I hadn't thought much about them, honestly. But I get what you're saying."

"Wow, thanks," I said.

Hearing my father, the Robert Lee I had always looked up to most, tell me that my words had made him consider how statues of our ancestor affect other people was a humbling moment for me. There's something about preaching to strangers that is impersonal. To preach to your family, son to father, is a wholly more complicated affair.

"I never really thought it was an issue that concerned me," he later told me, referring to the public display of Confederate monuments. "I knew it was important, but it didn't affect my day-to-day life until after Charlottesville." Learning that my message had gotten through moved me and gave me hope that what we see as normal today might not always be the case.

Back in the hotel, my phone was driving me crazy. Notifications alerted me to media requests. Twitter was filled with alerts, more angry messages. Though a few occasionally offered praise, I was frustrated. The focus, I tried to tell anyone who would listen, should be on the cause of racial reconciliation. Not on me, my family name, or my experience with my church. But it seemed no matter how much I tried to move the spotlight, it didn't bring much illumination.

And so, in what may not have been the most helpful way to diffuse the situation, I took to Twitter to let off some steam. "I dislike the line: 'Lee descendant leaves church,'" I wrote. "I'm Rob Lee and I haven't left the church. Y'all haven't gotten rid of me yet."

10

Throughout my life something
odd kept happening to me. God showed up.

—DIANA BUTLER BASS

W HERE IS GOD in these stories of transformation, reformation, and redemption? When I was in
seminary, Dr. Stanley Hauerwas, a professor at Duke, said
something that stuck with me.

"The same God who brought the Israelites out of Egypt
is the God who brought Jesus out of the tomb," he said.

Going a step further, I would add that this God, a God
of liberation, is the same God who is with us today. A God
who is deeply concerned and invested with the liberation
of the South and its history. To be deeply vested in such
liberation requires that we, the people of God, reteach
loveliness to the places where we live.

As I wrote this book, I sought input from my family,
neighbors, fellow believers, and even those who do not
share my views about the need for the South's redemption.

It's never easy to speak so honestly about a place that so many others call home. So I wanted to do something of a check-in, to make sure that I accurately captured the people who make the South the beautifully messy place that it is. I was heartened by some of the stories people shared with me, stories about racial harmony, neighbors helping one another out, and the inspiring role that faith continues to play in the lives of so many people here.

But at the same time, I was reminded of how much further we have to go. My friend David Crabtree summed it up nicely. For years, David was a television anchor at Raleigh's NBC affiliate, so he knows as well as anyone the heartbeat of the South. Not too long ago, he announced his plans to leave his job, pursue further theological studies, and seek a leadership role in the Episcopal Church. "Older white America, my generation, can't see our racism," he says. "We could pass a polygraph saying 'I'm not racist,' but what we need is a polygraph of the heart."

David is right. Even with the best intentions, white people who live in the South are unable to escape the subtle, and sometimes not so subtle, racism that drives so much of life here. For too long we've had a "progressive quietness" down here that seeks to soothe our fundamentalist and Evangelical siblings. Time and time again, I have failed to rise to the occasion of addressing the problematic narrative of racism. I have been complicit; I have been silent. I have been racist. Even with everything I hope I've learned, I still have such a long way to go.

Sometimes, even the most mundane of tasks forces me to confront my family's legacy and this regrettable fact of life in the South. Take a recent visit to a big-box home-improvement store.

Part of the spring ritual down here, in addition to loading up on allergy medication and wiping thick coats of pollen off our windshields, is getting the garden ready. A few months ago, Stephanie and I hopped in the car and made our way to the store, ready to stock up on hoses, flowers, and mulch for our new home.

As we finished up shopping and made our way to the cashier, only one thought was on my mind: Please, God, allow my allergies to let up enough for me to get some of this yard work done. I chatted idly with Stephanie as the clerk rang up the items. He told me the total and I handed him my bank card. Then the question came.

"You related to him?"

This wasn't the first time this has happened, and I no longer turn red and fumble with my answer like I used to.

"Yep," I usually say, hoping that will be the end of it. But it never is. The conversation then either goes one of two ways. My preferred sequence of events is that the admission elicits a curious, "Huh," allowing me to choose whether I'll offer more or to put the issue to bed. The second—the response that induces panic within me—happens when people see the name Robert Lee and think they've found a fellow fan.

This time, the cashier took the second approach.

"That's so cool," he said. "The South will rise again."

I smiled nervously, thinking he must be kidding. But I didn't engage. There was a line of customers behind us, and in that moment, it felt easier to simply get back to work.

Another time, the issue came up when I was in a doctor's office getting blood drawn.

"What's your name?" the nurse asked me.

"Robert Wright Lee IV," I responded, not thinking much of it.

She scanned my arm band. "What a cool name," she remarked.

"You don't know the weight of it," I said, perhaps imprudently, since at that very moment she was fiddling with a long needle that was about to go in my arm.

"I wish people would understand he was a good man," she said, avoiding eye contact with me—or maybe just focused on her task. I'm still scratching my head on that one. What do you say to someone who's sticking your arm with a needle while telling you your Confederate uncle was a good man?

These responses from strangers baffle me. The cashier's statement, "The South will rise again," has a racist undertone that makes me uncomfortable. I, too, hope the South thrives, but in a way that includes black folk and white folk and all of God's children together. There is little about the so-called Old South that deserves a resurrection.

Comments like the one from the nurse are a bit more

nuanced. Sure, it'd be great if everyone understood our history more thoroughly. In some areas, Lee was a good man, devoted to his family and his faith, serving his country for years as a brilliant military tactician. People who demonize him completely risk morphing him into a caricature, forgetting that he was a human being just like us, or falling into another common trap: thinking that just because we believe the right things about slavery or modern politics, we are incapable of racism ourselves. This is simply not the case. As the twentieth-century Russian writer Aleksandr Solzhenitsyn put it, "The line dividing good and evil cuts through the heart of every human being." It's important to remember this as we look at historical figures, and more important, at our own actions and motives.

More often than not, I feel painfully inadequate when I'm trying to have these deep conversations about race. We expect and hope that all our conversations about race will be enlightened and "woke," but ultimately, there will always be moments when you don't know what to say, how to handle it, or whether you should even engage at all. There are many times when I wish I'd spoken up more. I recognize this is a privileged statement for me, because I get to pick and choose when to engage. Our black siblings aren't always so lucky.

My friend Adam, who asked that I not use his last name, leads a small church down here in North Carolina. The church is still predominantly white, despite Adam's best efforts to make the congregation look more like the diverse community where it's located. This church is home to many players on the local high school's football team, which has struggled in recent years. In a part of the country where devotion to football is second only to devotion to God, suffice it to say that this has not been taken well.

One day after worship, a prominent member of the church approached the pastor. He told Adam that, in his opinion, the reason their football team loses so many football games is "because we do not have enough n—— playing on our team." Pressing his point further, he added that the rival team performs so well only "because they can 're-nig' up after every season."

"My mouth hit the floor," my friend recalled. "I told him we cannot talk this way and still consider ourselves Christians. I told him that this language is contrary to the family of God, and if you are going to use this language and sentiment, I will need you to leave our church."

Eventually, the pastor told me, the man apologized and returned to the church. Adam said that as a minister, he struggled with allowing the man to resume his leadership role in the church. As Christians, we should be as aware as anyone of the power of redemption. Still, it's not always easy. And Adam's story is a reminder that white people need to call out the hateful underlying prejudices that too often pass unchecked in private. There are few among my folk in the South who haven't been affected by systemic racism, and bringing this troubling aspect of our culture into the open—whether in a private conversation between a pastor and a worshipper, or in town hall–style conversations following painful events like those in Charlottesville—is never easy. But I have come to believe that the burden of reconciliation cannot fall to people of color. White people made this mess, and we must do our part to strive for healing.

After telling me his story, Adam made an observation about life in the South that has really stuck with me. Of course, it applies to American culture more broadly, but it's especially true down here.

"We love to section ourselves off with people who look like us, think like us, and worship like us," he told me. "I believe this causes us to never have conversations with people of color, with people who have a different economic status, with people who are Democrats or Republicans, with people who are differently abled, even with people who are different in age.

"I pray our churches will no longer look like sections," he continued. "Rather, I hope that the church can be messy. I pray that people in the church can truly say, 'Peace be with you,' to people they don't agree with or look like.

"My hope is that with the announcement of peace, people will begin to realize the love of God found in one another. I believe if we keep sectioning ourselves off, then the other will just look like a monster instead of a person who is the face of Christ."

Turning the other into a monster rather than an encounter with the Jesus of the Gospel is an apt description of what we in the South have done to one another for generations. But it doesn't have to be this way. The people in my life who have taken time to teach me this are proof that we can do better—and that we must.

DURING A RECENT visit to Chicago, I was invited to speak at a synagogue's Friday night Shabbat service by Rabbi Michael Siegel. After sharing my experiences with the congregation, I chatted with many of the folks gathered there. Listening to their stories of resiliency in the face of some of the greatest horrors of the twentieth century, I marveled at how the Jewish faith reminds adherents to pass on the stories of their ancestors to their children and their children's children. The Jewish people gathered for Shabbat dinner were not afraid to encounter the horrifying nature of the world's collective history, and consider how it affected them and continues to have an impact on them. We need only look back to the Holocaust and anti-Semitism that still rages amid white nationalists today to see the proof that silence is complicity. They needed people to speak up on their behalf and with them in solidarity when the world seemed to have forgotten them, abandoned them, or were ignorant to their plight. It reminded me of the "seventh generation principle" in the Iroquois tradition, which teaches that the decisions we are making now will affect our planet for seven generations to come. We have a choice. We can remain bystanders, complicit in our silence, or we can seek to be agents and effectors of change.

Plenty of well-meaning people have come to me after a sermon and said, "I just don't know if I can do it by myself; I don't know if it's worth it to stir the pot."

These are heartbreaking sentiments. There's a cost to speaking up, and people have real and honest reasons for choosing to stay silent. But I remember looking at the lectionary one Sunday as I was about to preach, and having a verse from that week's reading hit me like a train. In the Gospel of Mark it says, "What good is it if you gain the world, but forfeit your soul?"

I think it's time for some proverbial "pot stirring." It's time we change the way we talk about issues facing us here in the South. At a minimum, we have to be willing to start a dialogue that offers concrete evidence of what each side is thinking.

In 2016, a white C-SPAN viewer, "Garry from North Carolina," called into a program to talk to a guest, Heather McGhee, who was African American. The story went viral after the *Washington Post* picked it up.

Garry said simply, but bravely, "I am prejudiced." He explained that his prejudice had been fueled by a media diet that painted all black people as criminals, and that he was scared. He wanted to know what he could do to change. "You know, to be a better American?"

McGhee nodded along as Garry asked his question. Though it isn't the job of any African American to help white people be less racist, she gave a thoughtful answer.

"Thank you so much for being honest and for opening up this conversation, because it is simply one of the most important ones we have to have in this country," she said. She added that all people tend to harbor some biases, and that naming them aloud, in order to bring about change, is "one of the most powerful things that we can do right now in this moment in our history." She suggested that reading up on the history about race and getting to know black people could actually help. Garry promised that he would get to know McGhee herself.

A year later, in 2017, the *Post* reported that the pair eventually met, exchanged stories, and listened to each other. They are now friends, and Garry Civitello says his views on race have evolved, in part because he was willing to start the conversation by admitting his own prejudices and lack of expertise. "There are so many things I did not know that I thought I knew," he said.

Through conversations like these, we can come to an idea of how to solve the problems that are so prevalent and pertinent today. I don't claim to have all the answers for fixing the South, but I know that through dialogue and reconciliation we can begin a transformation that will lead us to new horizons and different frontiers of grace.

There are many battles still to be fought over Confederate statues and racism. There are many lines in the sand that will be crossed over white supremacy and white privilege. But if we're willing to express a desire to change here in the South, we can begin to seek the transformation of this nation and this world.

History will judge us based on how we responded to a post-Charlottesville America. We must summon the courage to confront our own relatives and friends and do the hard work of talking about these issues around the dinner table. We must engage in the conversation with an open heart and mind. We must be active listeners to persons of color, especially here in the South, regarding issues of racism and societal ills such as Confederate monuments.

The issue of monuments and statues continues to divide our nation. It's a question I'm asked in almost every public forum at which I find myself. I've had a lot of time to reflect on the question, and a story from the Bible keeps coming to mind. In Acts 19, Paul is on his way to Ephesus when Demetrius, a builder of statues of the goddess Artemis, becomes concerned that if Paul's religion spreads, no one will buy the statues he has spent so much time making. Fearing this threat to his business, Demetrius starts a riot and runs Paul out of town. Sound familiar? This story is about the fear of what might happen if things change. Had Demetrius not resisted the change Paul was offering, he may have lost everything he held dear—his money, his history, his way of life—but he also would have experienced the life-changing possibilities brought to him by God made known in Christ.

The same is true for us in our time. If we're serious about changing how the world sees the South, we must first admit that Confederate monuments are monuments of white supremacy and idols of racism. Then we must atone for the sin of racism by tearing down the monuments that have plagued our landscape for too long. We must say "Enough is enough."

As I've engaged in this work, I've had seminary class-mates and members of my community accuse me of grandstanding. I've been disinvited from churches, and two friends who participated in my wedding no longer talk to me. They accuse me of seeking the limelight, of using my experiences for notoriety's sake and not for the sake of the transformation of the world. It breaks my heart that transformation is costly, and yet I remain resolved. I remain resolved because there is nothing that could be unseen in this endeavor. I can't just roll back the tape and hope for better circumstances or do things differently. I can't take back the words I've said in public, even when the doubt creeps in and the anxiety resumes its march.

But I've gained much from of all this, as well. I've dis-covered new friendships and seen old ones rekindled—friends who have come to say it is well with our souls and that all will be well. That is a great gift that I cherish in spite of the loss. Being in public theology is incredibly iso-lating, and I feel it creeping into my mental health, but I know that God has called me to this particular moment in history for a purpose and a reason, and that there is something more to our existence than just sitting idly by as the world turns. In the time since I started in ministry, I've kept an eye open for signs of light. They aren't always easy to find. Sometimes, it feels like people committed to the cause run around in circles, unable to break through to the wider culture about the need to undertake this difficult work. But occasionally, there are signs of hope.

As I write this, officials in three states—Oklahoma, Missouri, and Virginia—are considering renaming schools named for Robert E. Lee. These cases are no-brainers, but like with the school in Texas I mentioned earlier, it isn't always easy. There are fights over culture, embedded prejudices, and structures of inequality that go deeper than the name of a building. But it's a start.

In Fort Myers, Florida, a group of brave activists are urging city leaders to remove a bust of Robert E. Lee from a busy downtown street. The statue is a nod to the name of the county where Fort Myers sits, but Lee County NAACP president James Muwakkil wants it to come down. In a fiery speech made before the Fort Myers City Council in May 2018, he said, "We all have mandates to address Confederate hate symbols wherever we see them."

Muwakkil is right—the statue in Fort Myers should come down, along with others like it across the South. But that's just a first step. Even when statues are removed, there is still work to do—sometimes a lot of work, as supporters of such displays feel besieged. But we can't avoid difficult decisions just because some people will be upset.

Please hear me when I say I know this is risky business. But even in my relatively short experience of ministry, I have found more people willing to say yes to God's dream than no. I met many of them not in the church, but through social media outlets, around dinner tables with friends, and even in unexpected holy moments that took place outside the four walls of a church building. Howard Thurman is famously credited with saying, "Don't be so heavenly minded that you do no earthly good." For too long, the church has existed as the gatekeeper to what is acceptable to the God we serve. Perhaps we could move into tomorrow with strong and certain hope that the Kingdom of God leaves no one behind.

In English class at Statesville High School, my teacher Wanda McConnell said that committing pen to paper is part of "showing up." We must show up, we must start the journey toward wholeness today. We can't wait any longer. For waiting ultimately costs lives, it costs the possibility of renewal, and it negates the long moral arc of the universe that has been bending toward justice for a long, long time. If enough pastors and laypeople spoke up about the issues of white privilege, supremacy, and racism, we would have a different world. We can no longer sit in complicity as white moderates. We must be forever moving into God's plan for our world, no matter the cost.

11

It's being willing to walk away that gives you
strength and power—if you're willing to accept the
consequences of doing what you want to do.

—WHOOPI GOLDBERG

FOLLOWING MY RESIGNATION from the
church in North Carolina, and the media attention it
brought, I was feeling lost, like my ministry was sunk and
I had no way forward. Then a childhood hero called. Or,
rather, a producer from *The View* emailed me on behalf of
Whoopi Goldberg, asking if I would appear on the show to
talk about the challenges facing the white church when it
comes to race. Feeling depleted from everything my family and I had endured, I wasn't quite ready to say yes. The
show wanted me to travel to New York for a Friday taping, but I asked Stephanie if we really wanted to keep taking part in this heated public conversation. What if I had

made my case, and now it was time to bow out? I could name dozens of people who deserved this platform more.

But I didn't want to close the door entirely. So I explained to the producer that I had to teach class and couldn't make it. I asked if they would mind rescheduling, half hoping that they would simply move on. But it wasn't in the cards. Sure, they said. Whoopi really wanted me on, and they would find a time to make it work.

We agreed on a date and booked flights to New York. But before going on the show, I knew I needed some deep spiritual nourishment, so I called the Reverend Stephen Green, a brilliant young pastor at Heard AME Church in Roselle, New Jersey. Stephen is a dynamic preacher and a respected leader in the racial justice movement. Early in his ministry, he worked as a national leader in the NAACP, mobilizing college students and helping to train young activists. At one point, he was arrested for staging a sit-in at the office of Senator Jeff Sessions, who had just been nominated to serve as attorney general under President Trump. More recently, he's led protests supporting Colin Kaepernick, the quarterback who's been blackballed by the National Football League for taking a knee during the national anthem to protest police violence.

When Stephen and I first met, I was immediately struck by his passion for reconciliation. We became friends and started following each other's work. Since I was heading up to New York, I knew I needed to see him, so I emailed

Stephen and asked if I could swing by his church on Sunday morning.

"Why don't you come preach!" he replied, making it sound more like a statement of fact than a question.

I wasn't looking for another speaking gig, but Stephen's persistence won over.

"Of course, I'd love to," I told him.

After the hassle of traveling from Charlotte to New York and then out to New Jersey, I felt far from ready to preach about racial justice. But as soon as I shook hands with Stephen, I felt more at ease. He is a natural pastor, able to make others feel comfortable and aware of God's presence in their lives. When he handed me a small gift—a T-shirt that said "God is Woke"—a smile broke out across my face.

"God may be woke, but am I?" I joked, the self-doubt returning at a not-so-opportune time.

But as the service began, the congregation—mostly people of color who knew far more intimately than I the challenges of race in this country—raised my spirits with a warm welcome and a rousing rendition of the hymn "Revive Us Again."

We praise thee, O God!
For Thy spirit of light,
Who hath shown us our Savior
and scattered our night.

The words stuck with me, reminding me that the chaos of darkness would ultimately be overwhelmed by the power of light. For a few moments, I felt a peace that had eluded me in recent months. Then, it was time to preach.

I am a young pastor, and the fallout from my work had shaken my confidence in my call. This particular morning, standing in front of a couple hundred people, dressed in their Sunday best and standing to applaud me before I had spoken a single word, I felt like a fraud. Who was I to be delivering this message? Who was I to offer a word of reconciliation to a group made up of predominantly people of color? For Christ's sake, my name is Robert Lee— and frankly these people knew far more about the Gospel and racial justice than I did, having lived it day in and day out for many decades. I was a white kid from the nice part of town who had hung a Confederate flag on his wall and who couldn't even keep a job at a small church. Who did I think I was?

But as I looked out at the crowd, who by now had taken their seats, I knew I had a job to do. I couldn't run, no matter how badly I wanted to. I closed my eyes, took a deep breath, and prayed, as I do before each sermon, that God would speak through me.

Then I delivered my sermon. I invoked the Bible passages we had read, recalled some of my experiences from the past few months, and asked for prayers from the congregation. The smiles I saw on many faces restored some of my confidence—both in myself and, more important, in the Christian church.

Following the service, I stuck around to greet some of the worshippers. This is one of my least favorite parts of these visits, if I'm being honest. I'm an introvert, and a bit shy when meeting new people. But that day was different. Worshippers greeted me warmly, shared pieces of their stories, asked me about my life, and joined in side conversations with one another. The small talk was pleasant and I was enjoying myself. But there was one man, whom I had noticed from the pulpit because he was one of the few white faces in the crowd, who seemed agitated. And he was making me uncomfortable.

Quickly and without warning, he rushed up to me, his face filled with anger.

"You're stirring up trouble," he barked, his eyes fixed on mine.

His words startled me. I was unsure how to respond. I had heard this phrase hurled at me in the South, but this was New Jersey—and in a predominantly black church! I tried to think of something to say, to help diffuse what I felt might be a tense situation. But before I could, one of the associate pastors said, "Don't worry, we've got your back." And with that, the man was guided out of the church.

Conversations about our disagreements are important, but true conversation dies in the presence of hatred and verbal threats. I was thankful to the crowd for stepping into an uncomfortable situation, especially when their own safety could have been placed at risk. Their words of encouragement reminded me that I have a role in this fight, that people are hungry for God's word, and that I should not give in to the voices of doubt and hate. I took that message to heart, and carried it with me to Manhattan the next day.

.

IT TURNED OUT that Whoopi had missed the taping of the episode I was originally invited to attend. This meant that if I hadn't balked at the invitation, I would have missed the opportunity to meet the woman who played one of my childhood icons on *Star Trek*. I laughed when I was told this, aware that God's sense of humor is often more playful than we allow for.

Just before the taping, I learned that my former church had hired a PR firm and lawyers to discredit my story. I found myself pacing in the green room in between makeup and production meetings. Two friends had accompanied me to the taping, and they told me that all would be well. I wasn't so sure, but I trusted their instinct.

On set, my nerves settled a bit. My goal had been to shift the conversation away from headlines like "Robert E. Lee's Nephew Forced to Resign from All-White Church" back to the more important topic of racial reconciliation, taking down Confederate statues, and atonement for the sins of white supremacy. This was the platform that God had given me, and I wanted to use it not to settle scores or rehabilitate my own image, but to shine the light on the challenges people of color face in this country every day. "This isn't about me," I remember telling myself right before I went on set. It never has been.

The segment began with a clip from the VMAs. Along with the audience, I watched the monitors, and I relived some of that night. Then I said a quick prayer that I'd find the right words to highlight the important work that others were already doing. Following a brief introduction, Whoopi asked me why I'd chosen to speak out about taking down Confederate monuments.

"Well, after Charlottesville my heart was broken," I replied. "If you're silent in these issues, you become complicit in these issues, and complicity is not something I stand for. I can only speak for myself. What I do know is that it's hard to stand for something. . . . I had to stand up and say this is what I believe in, and I'm going to stand by it."

The audience applauded. I was settling in. We may have been seated inside a television studio, but the room had a feeling not unlike a church.

Joy Behar, one of the more outspoken panelists, said that church, at its best, is supposed to be "a beacon of compassion."

I told her I agreed.

"White Christianity is having trouble dealing with what's going on in our nation today," I said. "We're having trouble talking about these issues of race, reconciliation, of reparations, of redemption. We have trouble finding the vocabulary to speak about these issues. But I want it to be said of me that there was a Lee in history who stood up for what is right, instead of a General Lee who stood up for something that is wrong."

More applause. The message was getting through.

"The pulpit is inherently political," I continued, encouraged by the response from the panel and crowd. "This is a way of combating racism and white privilege and white supremacy in the best way I know how, through my pulpit."

Whoopi gave me a shot of confidence when she said, "I tell you, I almost could go back to church to hear you talk. This is what it's supposed to sound like."

Then she spoke directly to my self-doubt, adding, "You can never stop talking."

So, I didn't. I kept going. And I still am.

The night after the taping, Whoopi emailed me to thank me for coming on the show. She signed it "Guinan," the name of her famous *Star Trek* character, the one who had prompted that conversation two decades ago with my dad. I showed Stephanie as soon as I read it, then called Dad to tell him Guinan had asked about him. The whole thing was surreal.

But what made that trip worth it was the outpouring of support from people who have spoken with me following the airing, talking about their own struggles with racial reconciliation. People really are grappling with hard questions that can't be answered with superficial platitudes. It would be easy for us to sit among our progressive circles and take pity on people who just "don't get it"—and there certainly are people who will *never* get it. But I know deep down that people across this great nation are trying to change, and sometimes it takes a push from unlikely places, like a collateral descendant of General Robert E. Lee appearing on *The View*.

The temptation to believe that we as individuals have no role in healing America's sin of racism is too powerful. It's demonic. I've been given a platform because of my family lineage, and because I was at the right place and ignorant enough to think I could make a difference. As I said on *The View*, I feel a sense of responsibility because of my name. But we all have a role to play, especially those of us who in our whiteness have a sanctuary from the ugliness of racism. It's easy to shield ourselves from the reality of race-based hatred in the United States. But our faith demands more. Our faith calls us to speak up, even when it is difficult. Especially when it's difficult. Anything less is complicity in sinfulness. We must resist.

12

Injustice anywhere is a threat to justice everywhere.
We are caught in an inescapable network of mutuality,
tied in a single garment of destiny.
Whatever affects one directly, affects all indirectly.

—THE REVEREND DR. MARTIN LUTHER KING, JR.

THIS BOOK, my letter of love to a place that has shaped me, and the place where my wife and I have chosen to live our lives, began with a reflection about a speech I delivered at a breakfast honoring one of my heroes, the Reverend Dr. Martin Luther King, Jr. So I think it's only fitting that it should end with another moment set aside to honor the slain civil rights leader. This time, the venue was not a convention center in my small hometown of Statesville, surrounded by family and friends. This one took place a year later, in Atlanta, at the church where Dr. King himself had preached.

The road to the King Center began with an email I received from a personal hero, the Reverend Dr. Bernice A. King, daughter of the late Martin Luther King, Jr., and

Coretta Scott King—and a civil rights icon in her own right. A staffer at the King Center wrote to tell me that Bernice King wanted to invite me to visit the center, meet with her, and consider taking part in their annual Martin Luther King, Jr., celebration in a few weeks.

"Absolutely, I'd love to," I wrote immediately.

On the way to Atlanta, my train was severely delayed, and the weather was stifling hot when I arrived. By the time I made it to the office, I was agitated and sweaty. But then Bernice walked out with a big smile on her face. My shoulders relaxed, and I forgot about my travel woes.

"I'm Rob," I said, sticking out my hand.

"No, I'm gonna hug you," she said. And she did.

I didn't say anything. I was starstruck. As director of the King Center, Bernice had long carried on the King legacy while also using her platform to shine a light on the good work of others. She engaged in difficult conversations, leveraging her name and renown to bring people together to strategize and promote reconciliation. She also supported young activists still unsure of their role in this team effort.

As we made our way into Bernice's office, I was moved by the fact that you could see the final resting place of both her parents from one of the windows. The symbolism was striking. Bernice and I chatted for several minutes, in a way that two friends would talk. We asked about each other's families, chatted about upcoming travel plans, and inquired about some of the projects we were undertaking.

We didn't spend time lamenting the vastness of the task at hand, or even strategize about how to collaborate on this shared mission. Instead, we simply encountered one another.

Looking back, I see the genius of Bernice at work here. A friendly exchange between an indirect descendant of a man who gave up his country to fight for the cause of slavery and the daughter of one of the world's great civil rights leaders was a miracle of its own. Real change would come through conversations like this one. Yes, political activism, changes to laws, and even the removal of statues will be important. But for most of us, Bernice's friendliness that day is the best example we have of how to engage in this work. Seek out those who are different, welcome them, and listen. We all have a part to play.

The meeting included an invitation to attend the King Center's MLK celebration that would be held later that month. I had just a few weeks to prepare, so I got right to work.

When the day finally arrived, I paused to take it all in. Ebenezer Baptist Church is the mother church for black Christians in Atlanta. The history and sense of purpose at this sacred place was almost overwhelming. The crowd was a bit larger than my MLK speech in Statesville the year prior, and the energy was intense. We were filled with expectation and hope for a brighter and better tomorrow.

Before taking the platform, I thought about everything that had happened over the past year. Graduating from seminary. Getting married to the love of my life. Getting my first call as a pastor in a state I love, only to lose that post in the fallout from Charlottesville. While much had happened between that experience and my invitation to preach at the Ebenezer Baptist Church, I had come to feel that all the sacrifices had been worth it—that, finally, I was where God intended for me to be.

Up on the dais with me were several people I have come to revere because of their work. There was the Reverend Dr. Bernice King, who has continued to preach justice like her parents before her; Bree Newsome, who in 2015 heroically removed the Confederate flag from the grounds of the South Carolina state house; and Dr. Raphael Warnock, the pastor of Ebenezer Baptist, whose work I first encountered when he preached at Duke. I felt so blessed to stand alongside these role models. Saint Irenaeus is credited with saying that the glory of God is a human being fully alive. That's how I felt on that day, fully alive. This was a moment of grace, a reminder that we are not beholden to our pasts, not prisoners to our namesakes.

Speaker after speaker offered rousing tributes to Dr. King's life and legacy, praising his calls to universal brotherhood but also not shying away from some of his more challenging teachings. Leading up to the event, I had decided that I would use my five minutes not just to praise King, but to preach in an act of homage to him.

Right before I went backstage, Mrs. Bertha joined me in prayer: "I claim victory for Rob in the strong name of

Jesus." A claim of victory, in the name of a Palestinian Jewish man who was removed from this earth by crucifixion, but brought near to us through his glorious resurrection.

I was staring down at the floor hundreds of miles away, but my hands were clasped with hers for dear life. I said a quick, silent prayer, then made my way backstage to preach.

On Good Friday, 1963, authorities in Birmingham, Alabama, took Dr. King and other activists into custody, afraid that their protests would rile up African Americans and their allies at the start of the Easter holiday. While in the city jail, Dr. King received a copy of a newspaper containing a letter written by eight white clergymen who disapproved of the civil disobedience practiced by King and his followers. Dr. King was incensed, unable to accept that Christians could accept the status quo, in which black people were denied their humanity because of the color of their skin. He wrote down his reaction, beginning with notes on the newspaper itself. The full letter made its way into newspapers and magazines and has become one of Dr. King's most enduring teachings. That morning, in the church that he once led, I quoted that letter. The congregation was thoroughly familiar with the words, but I wanted to proclaim them in this space, as much to encourage myself as anyone else.

"But the judgment of God is upon the church as never before," I read. "If today's church does not recapture the sacrificial spirit of the early church, it will lose its authenticity, forfeit the loyalty of millions, and be dismissed as an irrelevant social club with no meaning for the twentieth century. Every day I meet young people whose disappointment with the church has turned into outright disgust."

As those words from Dr. King sank in, I made the case that our nation is in need of a renewed commitment to the vision communicated in that letter.

"America today," I preached, "is in desperate need of another 'Letter from Birmingham Jail.' The white Christian church in the United States has, at best, become complacent in the quest for racial justice. At worst, it's become downright hostile to it. I've been sickened and saddened by the number of prominent Christian voices who have supported an administration that openly expresses its hostility to equality and signals support to white supremacists. I'm dismayed by the lack of prophetic witness in many of our churches, which remain sinfully segregated on Sunday mornings. Our black brothers and sisters cannot be expected to carry the burden of racial reconciliation alone. Too often, even well-meaning white allies place the burden of justice solely on the shoulders of others. I've been guilty of this all too many times. The white church in this country must do more to see the Gospel come alive."

FOLLOWING THE EVENT at the King Center, I've reflected on the place Stephanie and I have decided to call home. Statesville still has a luster for a white man like me, and I'm hoping that we can make sure that luster isn't just for white folk. Despite the challenges we face, here in the South but also more broadly as a country, I remain hopeful. In fact, as I was writing this book, the congregation at a church in Virginia named for General Lee decided to contribute to our nation's healing by changing its name to Grace Episcopal Church. I'm sure it was not an easy decision for them. Few choices are when they require us to reckon with our past. But they are essential and life giving. We need to make this kind of soul searching the norm.

I don't know what will come next for me. But I do know that the many moments of grace I've experienced firsthand around issues of race and justice are too frequent to be overshadowed by episodes of hate. Because of my distant ancestor, a complicated man, I've been given a brief opportunity to preach love over hate, reconciliation over division. And if I soon return to obscurity, I will keep using the gifts God gave me to live and preach the Gospel, however imperfectly, seeking to usher in the reign of God here on earth.

My "Uncle Bob," as my parents used to call him, will always be the most famous member of the Lee family.

Historians continue to seek understanding about his life and his legacy, and our country finally seems poised to have a conversation about how he should be remembered. I hope to be a footnote in the history of the Lee family, a member who did what he could to respond to God's call.

AS I WAS headed from Atlanta back to North Carolina, my phone buzzed. It was Bernice. I was rushing to make my plane, but I swiped open the message.

"Your presence spoke volumes and provided hope in the midst of a very crazy time with so many things being reminiscent of some aspects of the '50s and '60s," she wrote. "I look forward to working together to change the trajectory, especially of the white Church."

I had a plane to catch, another talk to prepare, and was utterly exhausted. The physical toll of this has been real. But as I read Bernice's message, I paused to reflect on the gravity of that moment. Despite all the pain that could be present between us—the daughter of a civil rights champion and a man descended from the greatest hero of people who thought they had a right to own people like her—we had somehow connected over a shared vision of justice for all. For me, this was an undeniable sign of God's grace, a reminder that good things can happen in this flawed place that shaped me, that there's a future for this place I've chosen to call home.

In the book of James there is a famous verse: "Faith without works is dead." So let my faith be my creed, my mission, and my resolve to make this little plot of land here in Statesville look just a bit more like the Kingdom of God. Stephanie has been painting walls, and I've been unpacking boxes. In the expectancy of a new home and a new chapter, I leave this with Mother Aleen's vision fulfilled. There was darkness, to be sure. But as John's Gospel says, there is a light shining in the darkness, and the darkness cannot overcome it.

In many ways, this story is just beginning. I've never claimed to have a magic bullet. But as I sit here writing this with tears streaming down my face, I reflect on how writing a memoir is an exercise in remembering, as the preacher James Howell once wrote, the moments in life when you were "struck from behind by God." My first sermon was about God's love for us. Now, at twenty-six, and still mighty young, I've realized that responding to that love means loving one another. If we accept that God loves each of us, then we must respond by structuring our relationships on a hope that the real answers to our existence are all bound up in the greater nature of the God we serve. We're all just walking each other home, as Ram Dass famously said.

I was recently sitting with my friend Sarah Heath, a theologian for whom I have immense respect. We were bemoaning the travel schedules, the loneliness, the hardship of doing theology and confronting racism, among other things, in such a public way. As we sat over our cans of Coca-Cola, it hit me that while I may not be living the dream I intended for my life, I know that I am being somewhat useful in bringing about the reign of God. We all are. We're all working to bring home the message of loveliness that has become so elusive in our polarized culture. Sarah finally remarked, "We need to keep this going; the days look rough but it's going to be okay."

I'm reminded that dreams, even the one that Dr. King professed on the steps of the Lincoln Memorial, might take different forms than we could have ever imagined. I wanted to be the preacher riding in on a white stallion with a sword drawn ready for homiletic action. But instead I've been riding in on a donkey wondering how the bills will be paid and how I can articulate a message of hope for people who so desperately need it. If I reflect on this carefully I see that the white stallion might be more like General Robert E. Lee's way of doing things, not the way Jesus did things and not the way I intend to do things.

This book and the experiences shared in it have shown me abundant and abiding grace, and I will lay my claim on that. As the Psalmist wrote, weeping may endure for the night, but joy comes in the morning. The sun is rising on a new tomorrow, a new American dream, a new Southern way of life. So that in all of this, God's will might be done in North Carolina and in the South as it is in heaven. Amen.

ACKNOWLEDGMENTS

A STORY OF transformation can take place only because of the community that surrounds the transformation. There are so many people to thank for this story of coming to terms with identity and reality. To Bertha Hamilton, words cannot begin to thank you for the challenge of transformation you issued to me during my confirmation. To my parents, Rusty and Sherrie, thanks for not shying away from the questions I had as a child, for loving Stephanie, Frank the poodle, and me with an abiding and steadfast love. To my grandparents, especially Barbara, thank you for your constant belief in me. To Scott, my little brother, your courage and faith gives me hope; thank you for always asking the good questions. To Peyton, thanks for putting up with the Lee family and especially Scott. To Stephanie, my wife and my light, you have sung to me the song in the heart of God and shown me the power of plumbing the depths of my own soul. Thank you for your belief in me, which has to work sometimes in spite of me.

To Frank and Lizzie, my miniature poodle friends, thank you for your unconditional love.

Some of my closest friends in this writing process have been those who have tirelessly encouraged me to continue to show up and speak up. They have traveled with me and alongside me on my adventures, and for that I can't thank them enough: Megan Berry, Katelyn Byng, Britney Toner, Kelsey Lewis, Ruwa Romman, Palmer Cantler, and Molly Wright.

To friends Jessi Lancaster, Sarah Heath, Tuhina Rasche, Victoria Dyer, Michele Gardner, Dr. Diana Butler Bass, Morgan Bell, Benjamin Burton, Parker Garrett, Grace Starling, and Marcus and Taylor Paige, who all continually reminded me of my true north in all of this: I couldn't have done it without your respective and unique encouragement. To my students and faculty colleagues at Appalachian State University, thank you, especially Dr. Jean DeHart, Dr. Janice Pope, and Dr. Carolyn Edy.

To clergy mentors Nathan Kirkpatrick, Michael Gehring, Jonathan Walton, Susan Sparks, Reginald Keitt, thank you for your kindness. To Rabbis Michael Siegel and Daniel Vaisrub, thanks is not enough.

To the saints who will have to get a copy in the hereafter, Abbey Tsumas, Mr. and Mrs. Robert W. Lee, Sr.,

John Lee, Janie Bowman, and Gilbert Hamilton: I can only hope I have made you proud with the words committed in these pages.

To Dr. Bernice A. King and the fine folks at the King Center, including Kennedy Mack: Thank you for your contributions to this work.

To MTV, especially Noopur, Chris, and Stephen: I could spill gallons of ink in gratitude to you all for helping me find a voice and gain a soul back.

To my team, Michael J. O'Loughlin, Roger Freet, Ory Owen, Anissa Thaddeus, Derek Reed, and David Kopp: Your constant belief in this project and your willingness to see it to fruition is a testament not to me but to your gifted selves. Thanks, too, to everyone else at Convergent who worked on this book: Tina Constable, Campbell Wharton, Megan Schumann, Nick Stewart, Ashley Hong, Lauren Cornman, Jessie Bright, and Norman Watkins. You are talented folks who have shown me what it means to work hard and bring something to life from a small and minute dream.

Finally, to Statesville and my home church, Broad Street United Methodist Church, the town and faith community that I have known since my borning cry at Iredell Memorial Hospital: You allowed and encouraged me to dive deep in the waters of my baptism, so that I might yearn for something deeper and better for your beloved citizens; I thank you for the opportunity to grow up and grow strong.